gluten free BY DESIGN

Wendy Longo, Kitty Neckerman, Susan Wagener,
Debbie Zungoli and Pat Zungoli

Outskirts Press, Inc.
Denver, Colorado

The opinions expressed in this manuscript are solely the opinions of the authors and do not represent the opinions or thoughts of the publisher. The authors represent and warrant that they either own or have the legal rights to publish all material.

gluten free By Design
Easy, Elegant Recipes for Everyone
All Rights Reserved
Copyright@ 2009 Wendy Longo, Kitty Neckerman, Susan Wagener, Debbie Zungoli and Pat Zungoli
V3.0

Cover design and divider graphics by Emily Benson. Authors' photograph by Bob Bellinger.

This book may not be reproduced, transmitted, or stored in whole or in part by any means, including graphic, electronic, or mechanical without the express written consent of the publisher, except in case of brief quotations embodied in critical articles and reviews.

Outskirts Press, Inc.
http://www.outskirtspress.com

ISBN: 978-1-4327-3389-6

Library of Congress Control Number: 2008940117

Outskirts Press and the "OP" logo are trademarks belonging to Outskirts Press, Inc.

Printed in the United States of America

Table of Contents

Introduction 5
Our Story 5
How to Read a Food Label for Gluten 7
Is It Gluten Free? 8
Shopping Tips 11
Menu Suggestions 13
Recipes
    Breakfast/Brunch 17
    Appetizers 31
    Soups 49
    Salads 71
    Sides 93
    Main Dishes 119
        Beef 123
        Lamb 132
        Poultry 133
        Pork 151
        Seafood 159
        Pasta 166
        Vegetarian 175
    Desserts 181
Index 215

Disclaimer: We have made suggestions for some brand-name gluten-free products. Since product contents change, **ALWAYS** read labels for the most current ingredient information. When in doubt, call the company or check their web site. The authors have no control over, and accept no responsibility for, product production practices or ingredient changes.

Introduction

Our goal in writing this cookbook is to demonstrate that gluten-free cooking can be straightforward and uncomplicated. If you follow simple guidelines and familiarize yourself with the ingredients that are problematic, the rest is just cooking. This cookbook will give you the tools needed to confidently prepare gluten-free meals that everyone who shares your table will enjoy whether on a restricted diet or not.

Celiac disease is an autoimmune disorder that attacks the small intestine when affected people consume gluten. Gluten is a protein found in wheat, barley, rye and sometimes oats, and products derived from them. A celiac's body responds to gluten by producing a toxic immune reaction that prevents the absorption of vital nutrients. Because the susceptibility for celiac disease is an inherited condition, several people in a family may be affected, and often symptoms of the disease are not present until damage to the digestive system has already occurred. Even small amounts of gluten in the diet of a person with celiac disease may be damaging. The number of people diagnosed with celiac disease is rising precipitously each year and often other health problems occur as a result.

Our story

We began as a group of five women who came together to write a fundraising cookbook for our local community theater. Each person volunteered because of her interest in food and theater. In the year it took to write that book, meeting almost every week, we became friends. During those early meetings, we discovered that several of us also had an interest in special diets, particularly gluten-free cooking. In fact, one of us is a long-time celiac who has been cooking gluten free for years.

While working on the theater cookbook we realized that between the five of us, we had wonderful recipes, which could be adapted easily for gluten-free cooking. Depending on the time of day we met, each working session always included something to eat: an appetizer or snack, salad, main course or dessert. Since we had a celiac in our group, each hostess designed her menu to accommodate the diet. It soon became apparent that with just a little knowledge, one could easily change almost any recipe to be gluten free. The key was knowing what needed to be changed!

We have spent the last two years doing just that - carefully working through each recipe to be sure it is gluten free and easy to prepare! We have cooked and sampled our recipes, enjoying the food as we worked to create this cookbook.

Our cookbook is a collection of easy recipes for entertaining. We chose entertaining as a focus because we recognize how intimidating it is to prepare food for someone on a special diet. We have worked hard to create a book that celiacs can use or give to their family and friends. Our vision is that the gluten-free guest can arrive at a table anywhere our book has been used, and sit down to a delicious, safe meal!

For celiacs or others already familiar with the gluten-free diet, we invite you to jump right in! Share these recipes with family and friends or give the book as a gift.

For those new to the gluten-free diet, we invite you to read the next few pages carefully. These easy guidelines will help you get started and will serve as a good reference as you cook our gluten-free recipes.

How to Read a Food Label for Gluten

Getting the gluten-free diet right is just a matter of (a) **knowing the ground rules** and (b) **becoming a careful product label reader**. The following information will enable you to do both with ease.

The Ground Rules:

1. People following a gluten-free diet must strictly avoid all gluten-containing grains. These are WHEAT, BARLEY, RYE AND OATS. Although oats in moderation are considered okay for most gluten-intolerant people, oat crops are generally contaminated by wheat due to current farming practices. Unless oats have been purchased from a certified wheat-free farmer, they must be avoided. Oat products from a certified wheat-free source typically are not found in most grocery stores, but can be special ordered.

2. All derivatives of these grains such as FLOURS and STARCHES must be avoided, including MALT which is derived from BARLEY.

3. Food labels must be checked EVERY time a product is purchased. Manufacturers can change ingredients at any time.

4. As of January 2006, new labeling laws in the United States require that the top eight food allergens appear on the label. WHEAT is included in the top eight but not barley, rye or oats. This means that any ingredient containing wheat must include the word "wheat" on the label. For example, graham flour will be listed on a label as "graham flour (wheat)" or "CONTAINS: WHEAT" will appear at the bottom of the label.

*Is It Gluten Free?**

A Basic Diet Guide for Celiacs
Follow the guidelines below and be on your way to a happy, healthy, gluten-free life.

YES: The Following Foods are Gluten Free

Foods made from non-gluten containing grains (and grain-like plants):

Corn in all forms (corn flour, corn meal, grits)
Rice in all forms (white, brown, basmati, and enriched)
Amaranth
Buckwheat (kasha)
Quinoa
Millet
Montina
Tef
Sorghum
Soy

The following baking products:

Arrowroot
Cornstarch
Guar
Xanthan gums
Manioc (tapioca flour)
Potato starch flour
Potato starch
Vanilla
Beans and legumes (and flours made from them)

The following ingredients:

Annatto
Glucose syrup
Lecithin
Maltodextrin
Oat gum
Plain spices
Silicon Dioxide
Starch
Food Starch
Vinegar (only malt vinegar contains gluten)
Citric, lactic and malic acids
Sucrose, dextrose, and lactose

The following foods:

Milk
Pure Butter
Real (not processed) cheese
Plain yogurt
Vegetable oils (including canola)
Plain fruits
Vegetables (fresh, frozen and canned)
Meat
Seafood
Eggs
Nuts (and flours made from them)

NO: The Following Foods are NOT Gluten Free

Wheat in all forms including:
- Spelt
- Kamut
- Triticale (combination of wheat and rye)
- Durum
- Einkorn
- Farina
- Semolina
- Cake flour
- Matzo (matzah)
- Couscous

Ingredients with "wheat" in the name including:
- Wheat starch
- Modified wheat starch
- Hydrolyzed wheat protein
- Pregelatinized wheat protein

Barley malt, which is usually made from barley and malt syrup including:
- Malt extract
- Malt flavoring
- Malt vinegar
- Commercial beer is made from gluten. Gluten-free beer is available from several companies.

Other items to avoid:
- Breaded or floured meat, poultry, seafood and vegetables
- Sauces made from wheat or marinated in a mixture that contains gluten such as some soy or teriyaki sauces
- Licorice
- Imitation seafood
- Nuts flavored with gluten-containing ingredients

Maybe: Some Foods Have Hidden Sources of Gluten
Always read the label when dealing with the foods listed here

"Real" (not processed) cheese is gluten free; processed cheese (spray cheese, for example) may contain gluten

Dextrin, which is rarely used, can be made from wheat; if so, it will be on the label. Plain maltodextrin is usually derived from potato or rice.

Distilled alcoholic beverages are gluten free because distillation removes the gluten. Infrequently, gluten-containing ingredients may be added after distillation.

Flavorings are often gluten free, but may contain wheat or malt; wheat would be on the label, but malt would not.

Oats in moderate amounts are safe for most celiacs. Some companies produce oats specifically for the gluten-free market.

Pharmaceuticals can contain gluten, although most are gluten free. Check with the pharmaceutical company, especially if you take the medication regularly.

Seasonings and mixes have not been officially defined so they could contain gluten. By law, companies have to list wheat if it is found in any ingredient.

Spices are gluten free. If there is no ingredient list on the container, it contains only the pure spice noted on the label.

Soy sauce is often (though not always) fermented from wheat. Read the label, front and back.

Other foods to watch:
Self-Basting Poultry
Broth, Soups and Bouillon
Dried Fruits
Salad Dressings
Candy
Marinades
Lunchmeats
Sauces
Communion Wafers
Flavored Milk Drinks

This material is not intended to provide medical advice, which should be obtained directly from a physician.

*Adapted from "Gluten-Free Living", the magazine for those who follow a gluten-free diet. Information at www.glutenfreeliving.com or 914-231-6361

Shopping Tips

We have designed our recipes to make shopping simple by eliminating highly processed ingredients that may be a problem. We recommend brands for some items to give you a starting point, but for most of these, you may find other brands that are also gluten free. Remember, though, even with recommended brands, **ALWAYS READ THE LABEL** because product manufacturers sometimes change ingredients or production practices.

Here are a few guidelines to help make shopping easier:

- ✓ Fresh products are the best choice whenever possible.

- ✓ Most companies are very responsive to consumer inquiries. If in doubt about an ingredient after reading the label, contact the company. Customer service personnel will quickly provide the correct answers to questions concerning their products.

- ✓ Pure spices are gluten free; some seasoning blends and mixes may contain gluten (for example, curry is a blend and may contain gluten); **ALWAYS READ THE INGREDIENT LABEL.**

- ✓ Whipped products such as cream cheese, margarine or butter blends may contain ingredients that are not gluten free.

- ✓ Labels on low-fat and light products should be carefully read.

- ✓ Gluten-free breads are usually found in the freezer case.

- ✓ Wheat free **DOES NOT MEAN** gluten free.

Menu Suggestions

Spring Feast
Boursin Cheese with Gluten-Free Crackers
Marinated Leg of Lamb
Roasted Potatoes with Garlic & Thyme
Orange Honey-Glazed Carrots
Garlic Balsamic Vinaigrette over Mixed Greens
Chocolate-Coated Peanut Butter Eggs
Strawberries Romanoff

Mother's Day Meal
Shrimp with Tangy Cocktail Sauce
Chicken and Artichokes
Roasted Asparagus with Parmesan
Mandarin Orange Salad
Fresh Strawberry Pie

Light Summer Meal
Shrimp Salad
Mozzarella, Tomato, Basil Salad
Sesame Toast Triangles with Garlic
Frozen Strawberry Delight

Summer Picnic
Marinated Grilled Flank Steak
Artichoke Rice Salad
Emerald Isle Salad
Hummus with Fresh Vegetables
Deep Dish Peach and Blueberry Crisp

Out-on-the-Grill
Salsa Bean Dip with Gluten-Free Chips
Turkey Tenderloins
Greek Potato Salad
Easy Spinach Salad
Quick Key Lime Pie

Fall Harvest Dinner
Curry Spice Dip with Fresh Vegetables
Swedish Meatballs in Cream Sauce
Artichoke and Avocado Salad with Lemon Vinaigrette
Nutty Brussels Sprouts
Apple Cranberry Pie

Thanksgiving
Brined Roasted Turkey
Dressing with Roasted Garlic and Apples
Sweet Potatoes with Orange Glaze
Sautéed Green Beans and Onions
Curried Fruit
Cranberry Salad
Pecan Pie with Rum
Spicy Pumpkin Pie

Winter Holiday Celebration
Hot Crab Cocktail Spread
Pork Medallions in Vermouth and Coriander
White Rice with Peas
Oven-Roasted Broccoli and Cauliflower
Waldorf Salad
Crème Brûlée

Hearty Winter Dinner
Pot Roast Soup with Fennel and Parsnips
Easy Spinach Salad
Gluten-Free Bread
Baked Carrot Cake Pudding

Fast Family Meal
Fire-Roasted Tomato and Beef Pasta
Avocado Grapefruit Spinach Salad
Easy Cherry Dessert

Comfort Meal
Simple Meatloaf with Bacon
Garlic Mashed Potatoes
Fresh Corn Salad
Quick Chocolate Sauce over
Gluten-Free Ice Cream

Elegant Luncheon
Gazpacho or Chilled Cranberry Soup
Tropical Chicken Salad
Cucumber Salad
Sesame Toast Triangles with Garlic
Strawberries Romanoff

Intimate Dinner for Two
Sake Marinated Filet Mignons
Creamy Horseradish Potatoes
Asparagus with Shiitake Mushrooms and Tarragon
Strawberry and Walnut Green Salad
Chocolate Merlot Truffles

breakfast & brunch

Breakfast and Brunch

Apple-Puffed Pancake Casserole

Bacon and Broccoli Quiche

Bacon, Leek and Shiitake Mushroom Quiche

Baked Tuna Melt Sandwiches

Banana Almond Muffins

Blueberry Muffins

Cinco de Mayo Omelet

Crabmeat, Broccoli and Mushroom Quiche

Ham and Eggs with Rice

Overnight French Toast

Whole Grain Waffles

Breakfast & Brunch

Apple-Puffed Pancake Casserole

6 eggs
1½ cups milk
½ cup almond flour
½ cup rice flour
3 tablespoons sugar

1 teaspoon pure vanilla extract
½ teaspoon salt
¼ teaspoon cinnamon
½ cup butter
3 apples, peeled, cored and thinly sliced
2 tablespoons brown sugar

Preheat oven to 425°. Mix eggs, milk, flours, sugar, vanilla, salt and cinnamon in blender. Melt butter in 13 x 9-inch baking dish in oven. Add apples to dish and return to oven until butter sizzles. Do not brown! Remove dish from oven and pour batter over apples. Sprinkle with brown sugar. Return to oven, bake 20 minutes, and serve immediately. Serves 4

Notes:

BREAKFAST & BRUNCH

Bacon and Broccoli Quiche

Crust:

2 cups almond flour
6 tablespoons butter, melted

1 egg yolk, beaten

Butter bottom and sides of 9-inch pie plate completely. Place almond flour in bowl, add butter and blend with fork or pastry blender. Add egg yolk and combine well. Pour crust crumbs into pie plate and gently spread, covering bottom and sides. Once crumbs have been evenly distributed, press into place, smoothing top edge. Refrigerate until ready to use.

Quiche:

1 tablespoon extra-virgin olive oil
1 shallot, finely chopped
¾ cup yogurt (not fat-free)
3 eggs, beaten
8 ounces cottage cheese, drained*

¼ teaspoon basil
⅛ teaspoon nutmeg
4-6 strips bacon, cooked and crumbled
1 cup broccoli florets, steamed

Preheat oven to 350º. Heat oil in small pan and sauté shallots. Blend together yogurt, eggs, cottage cheese, basil, nutmeg and shallots in bowl.

Sprinkle bacon pieces and broccoli florets over bottom of crust. Pour yogurt mixture over top and distribute evenly.

Bake quiche 40 minutes or until lightly browned. Serves 6

A mild hard cheese may be substituted for cottage cheese; shred fresh cheese and sprinkle over broccoli and bacon.

Notes:

BREAKFAST & BRUNCH

Bacon, Leek and Shiitake Mushroom Quiche

This is a delicious quiche which eliminates milk and cheese without sacrificing flavor and texture.

1 (9-inch) gluten-free pie crust, unbaked
  (see beginning of Desserts for recipe)

Prepare and refrigerate pie crust.

Filling:

1 ounce dried shiitake or porcini mushrooms	Salt and pepper to taste
4-5 slices bacon	3 eggs
3 tablespoons butter	¾ cup soy creamer
2 pounds leeks, trimmed, washed and sliced	Dash nutmeg

Cover mushrooms with hot water and soak until soft, about 20 minutes. Strain, rinse and drain well. Chop into small pieces.

Fry bacon until crisp. Discard fat. Cool bacon slices on paper towels and chop into small pieces. Set aside.

Melt butter in large skillet. Add leeks, salt and pepper. Cover and cook 15 minutes, stirring often. Add mushrooms and continue cooking until leeks are soft but not brown, about 5 minutes more. Place leek mixture in large bowl and cool.

Preheat oven to 350º. Combine eggs, soy creamer and nutmeg in small bowl. Blend well and combine with leek mixture. Sprinkle bacon pieces on bottom of crust. Pour leek mixture over bacon. Place quiche in oven and bake until just starting to brown on top and knife inserted in center comes out clean, about 50 minutes.

Remove from oven, cool on rack at least 15 minutes and serve. Serves 6

BREAKFAST & BRUNCH

Baked Tuna Melt Sandwiches

*Lemon Mustard Vinaigrette**

1 garlic clove, minced
¼ teaspoon salt
1 hardboiled egg yolk

2 tablespoons lemon juice
1 teaspoon Dijon mustard
5 tablespoons extra-virgin olive oil

Blend minced garlic, salt and egg yolk using fork. Add lemon juice and mustard, and blend well. Add oil and stir until well combined.

Many bottled gluten-free dressings will also work: Italian or Ranch are good choices.

Sandwiches:

3 tablespoons butter, softened
8 slices gluten-free bread*
2 (6-ounce) cans tuna fish, drained
¼ cup lemon mustard vinaigrette, or to taste

2 cups broccoli florets, steamed
8 ounces mild cheese, sliced
2 green onions, chopped

Preheat oven to 400º. Spread softened butter on one side of bread. Place tuna in small bowl, add vinaigrette and blend.

Cut four pieces of foil, large enough to wrap sandwich easily. Place one slice of bread, buttered side down, on each piece of foil. Cover each bread slice with tuna mixture, layer with broccoli and cheese, and sprinkle with green onions. Cover each sandwich with remaining bread slice, buttered side up. Wrap each sandwich with foil, crimp and place on baking sheet. Bake 15-20 minutes. Serves 4

Gluten-free bread is found in the freezer section.

Notes:

Breakfast & Brunch

Banana Almond Muffins

A good blend of flavors

3 medium-sized bananas, peeled
4 eggs
½ cup honey
2 teaspoons pure vanilla extract
½ cup butter, melted
7¼ cups almond flour, divided

½ teaspoon salt
½ teaspoon nutmeg
1 tablespoon baking powder
1 teaspoon baking soda
1 cup walnuts, chopped

Preheat oven to 335° (yes, 335°). Line muffin pans with paper liners. Place bananas in bowl and mash using electric mixer. Add eggs, honey and vanilla. Blend well. Add melted butter to mixture with mixer running. Add half of almond flour, salt, nutmeg and blend. Add baking powder, baking soda and remaining almond flour. Blend well. Stir in walnuts.

Spoon batter into paper liners, until slightly rounded. Muffins will rise, but only a small amount. Bake 30 minutes. Muffins are done when center springs back when gently pressed. Edges will be lightly browned.

Cool 15 minutes before removing muffins from pan, cooling completely on racks. To store, freeze muffins. Makes 18 medium-sized muffins

Notes:

BREAKFAST & BRUNCH

Blueberry Muffins

2 cups blueberries
6 eggs
¾ cup honey
2 teaspoons vanilla extract
½ cup butter, melted

6¼ cups almond flour, divided
½ teaspoon salt
¼ teaspoon nutmeg
1 tablespoon baking powder
1 teaspoon baking soda

Preheat oven to 330º (yes, 330º). Line muffin pans with paper liners. Rinse blueberries and drain well. If blueberries have been frozen, use warm water to rinse and thaw. Do not place frozen blueberries into batter as that will slow down baking time.

Place eggs in bowl and blend with mixer. With mixer running, add honey, vanilla and melted butter. Then add half of almond flour, salt and nutmeg. Add baking powder and baking soda. Mix in remaining almond flour, blending all ingredients well. Stir in blueberries.

Spoon batter into muffin liners until slightly rounded. Bake 30 minutes. Makes 18 muffins

Notes:

BREAKFAST & BRUNCH

Cinco de Mayo Omelet

A spicy omelet, tasty every day of the year

1 teaspoon extra-virgin olive oil
¼ cup ham, chopped
2 tablespoons onion, chopped
2 tablespoons green pepper, chopped
2 eggs

1 tablespoon cold water
2 tablespoons tomatoes, chopped
¼ cup salsa
¼ cup fresh cheddar cheese, freshly shredded

Heat oil over medium-high heat in 8-inch non-stick skillet. Add ham, onions and green peppers, and sauté 5 minutes. Beat eggs and water in small bowl. Add to skillet and reduce heat to medium. With spatula pull the sides of omelet toward center and tilt skillet to allow uncooked portions to run to sides. When almost set, spread tomatoes, salsa and cheese over half of omelet. Omelet is cooked when bottom is lightly browned. Slide omelet onto plate, folding in half. Serves 1

If making more than one, keep omelet hot in 175° oven until all are done. To double recipe, use 10-12-inch skillet.

Notes:

BREAKFAST & BRUNCH

Crabmeat, Broccoli and Mushroom Quiche

A perfect Sunday lunch

1 deep-dish gluten-free pie crust (see beginning of Desserts for recipe)
2 eggs, slightly beaten
2 tablespoons rice flour
1 small onion, diced
½ cup mayonnaise*
½ cup milk
8 ounces Swiss cheese, freshly grated
¼ teaspoon salt
⅛ teaspoon freshly ground black pepper
Enough broccoli and/or mushrooms to add to crabmeat to equal 1½ cups total
1 cup crabmeat**

Preheat oven to 350º. Mix eggs, flour, onion, mayonnaise, milk, cheese, salt, pepper, vegetables and crabmeat, and pour into pie crust. Bake 45 minutes until golden brown. Cool 15 minutes before cutting. Serves 6-8

*Kraft and Hellmann's are gluten free.
** Do not use imitation crabmeat. It contains gluten.

Ham and Eggs with Rice

This is comfort food and a wonderfully easy recipe to prepare any time.

1 tablespoon extra-virgin olive oil
1 tablespoon butter
4 eggs, beaten
8 slices ham, chopped
2 green onions, chopped
1 cup frozen peas, cooked and drained
2 cups rice, cooked

Melt oil and butter in large skillet over medium heat. Add eggs and scramble. Immediately add ham, green onions and peas, stirring to combine and heat well. Stir rice into mixture and heat. Serves 4

BREAKFAST & BRUNCH

Overnight French Toast

Visit with weekend guests while breakfast is baking.

6 slices gluten-free bread*
2 tablespoons butter, melted
3 eggs
1 cup milk
2 tablespoons sugar
⅛ teaspoon nutmeg

⅛ teaspoon cinnamon
1 teaspoon vanilla extract
½ teaspoon salt
Gluten-free cooking spray
Powdered sugar (optional)
Topping of choice

Butter one side of each bread slice. Arrange buttered side up in ungreased baking dish just large enough to hold slices. Beat eggs, milk, sugar, nutmeg, cinnamon, vanilla and salt in small bowl until well blended. Pour egg mixture over bread slices. Cover and chill overnight.

Preheat oven to 350°. Remove bread slices from baking dish and place on sprayed baking sheet. Bake uncovered 35 to 40 minutes, or until golden. Dust with powdered sugar just before serving, if desired. Serve with any appropriate topping. Serves 3-6

For 8 slices of bread, increase number of eggs to 4, milk to 1¼ cups, and make all other measurements "rounded" or "heaping".

*Gluten-free bread is found in the freezer section.

Notes:

Breakfast & Brunch

Whole Grain Waffles

3 eggs, beaten
1½ cups milk or soymilk
¼ cup canola oil, corn oil or butter
1 teaspoon pure vanilla extract
1 cup almond flour
⅓ cup brown rice flour

⅓ cup millet flour
3 tablespoons quinoa flour
2 tablespoons ground flaxseed
1 teaspoon baking powder
½ teaspoon baking soda
¼ teaspoon salt

Preheat waffle iron. Beat eggs in medium-sized bowl. Add milk, oil, vanilla and blend.

Place flours, flaxseed, baking powder, baking soda and salt in large bowl. Blend well.

Pour wet ingredients into dry ingredients, using wire whisk or fork to blend well. Let batter sit 5 minutes to thicken. Makes 5 large waffles

Notes:

Notes

appetizers

Appetizers

Bacon Cheese Spread
Black Bean Hummus
Boursin Cheese
Cheddar Cheese Dip
Chili Pepper Peanut Dip
Clam Dip
Cocktail Swedish Meatballs
Creamy Taco Dip with Lime
Curry Spice Dip
Fresh Fruit Dip
Fruit Cocktail with Sherry
Guacamole
Hot Artichoke Soufflé
Hot Crab Cocktail Spread
Hummus with Fresh Vegetables
Mushroom Pecan Ball

Pineapple Cream Cheese Spread
Red Pepper and Garlic Dip
Salsa Bean Dip
Sesame Toast Triangles with Garlic
Shrimp Dip
Shrimp with Tangy Cocktail Sauce
Spicy Baked Olives
Strawberry Cheese Spread
Sweet and Sour Water Chestnuts

APPETIZERS

Bacon Cheese Spread

Easy and tasty – best served warm

6 ounce block sharp or extra-sharp cheddar cheese, cut in thirds
4 strips bacon
¼ cup onion, coarsely chopped
4 slices gluten-free bread*

Heat oven to 400°. Blend cheese, bacon and onion in food processor. Spread mixture on gluten-free bread. Bake 10 minutes. Cut into quarters and serve.

*Gluten-free bread is found in the freezer section.

Black Bean Hummus

A different flavor for an old favorite

1 (16-ounce) can black beans, drained
1 tablespoon sesame-seed purée (Tahini)
3 teaspoons extra-virgin olive oil
Juice of one lime
2 garlic cloves, minced
Salt and freshly ground pepper to taste
1 teaspoon ground cumin
Gluten-free tortilla chips or fresh vegetables

Combine black beans, sesame-seed purée, olive oil, lime juice, garlic, salt, pepper and cumin in food processor or blender. Process until smooth and transfer to serving dish. May be covered and refrigerated until ready to use. Bring to room temperature before serving. Serve with gluten-free tortilla chips or fresh vegetables. Makes 1½ cups

Notes:

APPETIZERS

Boursin Cheese

A great appetizer to have on hand for unexpected company

8 ounces cream cheese, softened
2 sticks butter, softened
½ -1 teaspoon dill
2 garlic cloves, pressed
¼ teaspoon marjoram
¼ teaspoon thyme
¼ teaspoon basil
2 tablespoons fresh chives, chopped
Freshly ground black pepper to taste
Onion salt and parsley (optional)
Gluten-free crackers or vegetables

Place softened cream cheese and butter in bowl. Add dill, garlic, marjoram, thyme, basil, chives, pepper, onion salt and parsley. Beat with mixer until smooth and creamy. Mold or place in crock. Chill and serve with gluten-free crackers. Make day or two ahead so flavors have chance to blend well. Will keep 4–6 weeks in tightly sealed container in refrigerator.

Cheddar Cheese Dip

Great for an impromptu gathering or delicious over steamed cauliflower and broccoli for dinner.

16 ounce block medium cheddar cheese
1 small onion, finely grated
15 ounces mayonnaise*
Gluten-free tortilla chips

Heat oven to 350°. Cut cheese into small pieces, and add onion and mayonnaise. Mix well, place in casserole dish and bake 30 minutes. Serve warm with gluten-free tortilla chips.

*Kraft and Hellmann's are gluten free.

Notes:

APPETIZERS

Chili Pepper Peanut Dip

This dip is great on a hot summer day and will stay fresh for hours.

1 cup unsweetened peanut butter
3 green onions including greens, coarsely chopped
½ cup fresh cilantro, chopped
1 jalapeño pepper, seeded and chopped
1 tablespoon soy sauce*
Juice of 1 lime
½ teaspoon turmeric
Warm water, as needed
Fresh vegetables

Place all ingredients, except water and vegetables, in food processor and blend until smooth. If mixture seems too thick, add warm water. Adjust amount of lime juice and soy sauce to taste. Serve with fresh vegetables.

*La Choy and San-J are gluten free.

Clam Dip

This is an old family favorite.

1 (6-ounce) can minced clams
1 tablespoon Lea and Perrins Worcestershire Sauce
8 ounces cream cheese, softened
Gluten-free crackers or fresh vegetables

Drain half the juice from clams. Add clams, remaining juice and Worcestershire Sauce to cream cheese. Stir until well mixed. Serve with gluten-free crackers or fresh vegetables.

Notes:

APPETIZERS

Cocktail Swedish Meatballs

1½ pounds ground pork
1 pound ground chuck
1 cup fine gluten-free bread crumbs (see beginning of Sides for recipe)
½ cup slivered almonds, browned in butter
2 eggs
3 tablespoons soy sauce*

2 garlic cloves, minced
Salt
Dash Tabasco
Dash nutmeg
Cornstarch
Extra-virgin olive oil

Combine pork, beef, bread crumbs, almonds, eggs, soy sauce, garlic, salt, Tabasco and nutmeg. Mix well. Form mixture into small balls (about 1-inch in diameter). Roll each in cornstarch. Fry balls in oil about 20 minutes.

Sauce:

½ cup white vinegar
½ cup water
½ cup sugar
4 tablespoons cornstarch

½ cup soy sauce*
1 (20-ounce) can pineapple chunks with juice

Mix vinegar, water, sugar, cornstarch and soy sauce. Cook over medium heat in saucepan 10 minutes. Warm meatballs, add to sauce, and stir in pineapple.

La Choy and San-J are gluten free.

Notes:

APPETIZERS

Creamy Taco Dip with Lime

A refreshing companion for fresh vegetables or gluten-free tortilla chips

8 ounces cream cheese, softened
8 ounces sour cream, room temperature
4-5 tablespoons McCormick taco seasoning
2 tablespoons fresh lime juice
Fresh vegetables or gluten-free tortilla chips

Mix all ingredients together except fresh vegetables or tortilla chips until well blended. Serve with fresh vegetables or gluten-free tortilla chips.

Curry Spice Dip

A spicy dip for fresh vegetables

2 cups mayonnaise*
1 garlic clove, minced
1 tablespoon McCormick curry powder
1 teaspoon fresh lemon juice
1 teaspoon Lea and Perrins Worcestershire Sauce
½ teaspoon freshly ground black pepper
½ teaspoon celery salt
Dash Tabasco
Fresh vegetables

Mix together mayonnaise, garlic, curry, lemon juice and Worcestershire Sauce. Add pepper, celery salt and Tabasco. Mix thoroughly and refrigerate. Serve with fresh vegetables. Makes 2 cups

*Kraft and Hellmann's are gluten free.

APPETIZERS

Fresh Fruit Dip

Perfect for dipping with strawberries, apples, oranges, grapes and melons.

1 jar Kraft Jet-Puffed Marshmallow Crème
8 ounces cream cheese, softened

Fresh fruit for dipping

Mix Marshmallow Crème and cream cheese until smooth and fluffy. Chill. Serve with fresh fruit.

Fruit Cocktail with Sherry

A refreshing starter for a summer meal

2 cups cantaloupe balls
1 cup honeydew balls
1 cup watermelon balls
1 cup seasonal berries

3 tablespoons honey
2 tablespoons lemon juice
2 tablespoons sherry
Mint sprigs for garnish

Combine all ingredients except mint. Chill. Serve garnished with mint sprigs. Serves 8 - 10

Notes:

APPETIZERS

Guacamole

Combines salsa and citrus for a tangy guacamole

6 medium or 4 large avocados
½ cup red onion, minced
1-2 garlic cloves, minced
Juice of 1 orange
Juice of 1 lime

3-4 cups salsa, drained
1 teaspoon freshly ground black pepper
Tabasco to taste
Salt to taste
Gluten-free tortilla chips

Peel avocados and mash. Add onion, garlic, juices from orange and lime, salsa, pepper, Tabasco and salt to avocados and mix. Adjust seasonings to taste. Serve with gluten-free tortilla chips.

Hot Artichoke Soufflé

Easy and elegant - can be made ahead of time and baked just before company arrives.

1 (14-ounce) can artichoke hearts, finely chopped
1 large garlic clove, minced
6-8 ounces Parmesan cheese, freshly grated
1 cup mayonnaise*

Dash Tabasco
Dash salt
Gluten-free crackers

Heat oven to 350°. Mix all ingredients together in an oven-proof dish, except crackers. Bake 30 minutes. Serve warm with gluten-free crackers.

* Kraft and Hellmann's are gluten free.

APPETIZERS

Hot Crab Cocktail Spread

An elegant beginning to any dinner party

8 ounces cream cheese, softened
1 tablespoon milk
2 teaspoons Lea and Perrins Worcestershire Sauce
1 cup fresh lump crab meat*

2 tablespoons green onions, chopped
Slivered almonds, toasted
Gluten-free toast points** or gluten-free crackers

Preheat oven to 350°. Combine cream cheese, milk and Worcestershire Sauce. Add crabmeat and green onions. Place mixture in small baking dish and top with slivered almonds. Bake 15 minutes. Serve warm with gluten-free crackers or toast points.

Do not use imitation crabmeat. It contains gluten.
**Gluten-free bread is found in the freezer section.*

Hummus with Fresh Vegetables

Also great in a wrap - spread on corn tortillas with tomatoes, lettuce, avocado, grated carrots and chicken

2 large garlic cloves, peeled
¼ teaspoon salt
1 (15-ounce) can chickpeas, rinsed and drained
⅓ cup sesame seed paste (Tahini), well-stirred

½ teaspoon ground cumin
2 tablespoons lemon juice
2 tablespoons extra-virgin olive oil
¼ cup parsley leaves
Salt and pepper to taste
Fresh vegetables or gluten-free tortilla chips

Mash garlic with salt. Place garlic paste in food processor with chickpeas, sesame seed paste, cumin, lemon juice and olive oil. Blend until smooth. Add parsley leaves, salt and pepper, and pulse until just combined. Serve with fresh vegetables or gluten-free chips.

Notes:

APPETIZERS

Mushroom Pecan Ball

Great for entertaining - more flavorful if made a day ahead

4 ounces fresh mushrooms, finely chopped
1 teaspoon butter or extra-virgin olive oil
8 ounces cream cheese, softened
1 teaspoon Lea and Perrins Worcestershire Sauce

2 teaspoons onion, finely chopped
Pinch salt
1 cup pecans, finely chopped
Gluten-free crackers

Sauté mushrooms in butter or oil. Drain mushrooms and allow to cool. Beat cream cheese until fluffy. Mix together all ingredients, except pecans and crackers. Form into ball and roll in pecans. Refrigerate. Serve with gluten-free crackers.

Pineapple Cream Cheese Spread

1 (8-ounce) can crushed pineapple, drained
8 ounces cream cheese, softened
2 green onions, finely chopped
1 small green bell pepper, finely chopped

¼ teaspoon salt
⅓ cup pecans, toasted and chopped
Parsley sprigs for garnish
Gluten-free crackers

Combine pineapple, cream cheese, green onions, bell pepper, salt and pecans. Chill. Garnish with parsley and serve with gluten-free crackers.

Notes:

APPETIZERS

Red Pepper and Garlic Dip

A creamy dip for fresh vegetables

1 large garlic clove, minced
4 ounces roasted red peppers, drained and diced
½ teaspoon red wine vinegar
⅛ teaspoon cayenne pepper
½ cup mayonnaise*
Salt and pepper to taste
Fresh vegetables

Place garlic, red peppers, vinegar and cayenne pepper in food processor. Process until mixture is well combined. Scrape mixture into bowl and stir in mayonnaise. Add salt and pepper. Cover and refrigerate at least 30 minutes to allow flavors to blend. Arrange assortment of fresh vegetables on platter and add dip when ready to serve.

* Kraft and Hellmann's are gluten free.

Notes:

APPETIZERS

Salsa Bean Dip

Starburst design makes a beautiful presentation.

4 green onions, cut into 1½-inch pieces
2 garlic cloves, peeled
½ teaspoon ground cumin
½ teaspoon salt
2 tablespoons fresh parsley
¼ teaspoon chili powder
2 (15.5-ounce) cans cannellini beans, rinsed and drained
¼ cup mayonnaise*
¼ cup lemon juice
½ cup salsa, drained
Dash Tabasco (optional)
Garnish: fresh cilantro sprigs
Gluten-free tortilla chips

Process green onions, garlic, cumin, salt, parsley and chili powder in food processor until coarsely chopped. Add beans, mayonnaise and lemon juice, and process until smooth. Spoon mixture into shallow 9-inch round dish making an indentation in center.

Process salsa until smooth. Spoon salsa into center of bean mixture. Pull tip of teaspoon through salsa toward edge of dish to create starburst design. Serve with gluten-free tortilla chips.

* Kraft and Hellmann's are gluten free.

Notes:

APPETIZERS

Sesame Toast Triangles with Garlic

Serve as an appetizer or with a favorite Italian meal.

2 tablespoons sesame seeds
¼ cup butter, softened
¼ teaspoon garlic powder
Dash cayenne pepper
½ cup Parmesan cheese, freshly grated
8 slices gluten-free bread*, crusts removed

Preheat oven to 375°. Toast sesame seeds on cookie sheet 4-5 minutes. Set aside to cool. Mash butter with fork and blend in sesame seeds, garlic powder and cayenne pepper. Stir in cheese. Spread mixture on bread. Cut bread in half diagonally to form triangles and place on cookie sheet. Bake 12-15 minutes or until toasted. Serves 8

Gluten-free bread is found in the freezer section.

Shrimp Dip

Wonderful as dip or sandwich spread

8 ounces cream cheese, softened
⅓ cup mayonnaise*
1 teaspoon fresh lemon juice
½ teaspoon onion, minced
½ teaspoon Lea and Perrins Worcestershire Sauce
2 tablespoons white wine
1 cup cooked shrimp, chopped
Gluten-free crackers

Mix all ingredients except crackers. If not consistency desired, add a little more wine or mayonnaise. Best if made at least half a day ahead. Refrigerate until ready to serve. Serve with gluten-free crackers.

Kraft and Hellmann's are gluten free.

Notes:

APPETIZERS

Shrimp with Tangy Cocktail Sauce

A simple, refreshing and delicious cocktail sauce

1 lemon, cut in half
¾ cup ketchup
3 tablespoons creamy, prepared horseradish*

1 teaspoon Lea and Perrins Worcestershire Sauce
½ teaspoon Tabasco
1 pound raw shrimp** (in shell)

Sauce:

Make sauce 1 hour to one day in advance of serving. Squeeze 1 tablespoon of lemon juice from lemon half. Combine lemon juice, ketchup, horseradish, Worcestershire sauce and Tabasco. Chill.

Shrimp:

Add both lemon halves to large pot of boiling salted water. Add shrimp and cook uncovered 3 minutes. Do not overcook. Remove with slotted spoon to bowl of ice water to immediately stop cooking. When shrimp are cool enough to handle, peel and devein. Keep cold until ready to serve with chilled cocktail sauce.

*Check the label – not all horseradish is gluten free.
**Pre-cooked, frozen shrimp also works well.

Spicy Baked Olives

Fills the kitchen with a wonderful aroma

2 cups assorted olives
2 tablespoons extra-virgin olive oil
1 teaspoon dried rosemary, crushed

1 teaspoon curry powder
1 teaspoon garlic powder
¼ teaspoon crushed red pepper

Preheat oven to 400°. Mix olives with remaining ingredients in oven-proof dish. All spices may be increased according to taste. Cover and bake 30 minutes.

APPETIZERS

Strawberry Cheese Spread

A bright and colorful appetizer; double this one - your guests will want more.

- 8 ounce block sharp cheddar cheese, freshly grated
- ½ cup mayonnaise*
- 3-4 green onions, finely chopped
- ⅛ teaspoon salt
- ⅛ teaspoon pepper
- ¼ teaspoon ground red pepper
- ½ cup pecans, toasted and chopped
- 1 (10-ounce) jar Polaner strawberry preserves
- Gluten-free crackers

Beat cheese, mayonnaise, onions, salt, pepper and red pepper at medium speed until blended. Stir in pecans. Place in mold, cover and chill 6-8 hours. When ready to serve, turn out of mold and spread with preserves. Serve with gluten-free crackers.

Kraft and Hellmann's are gluten free.

Sweet and Sour Water Chestnuts

A tasty blend of contrasting flavors

- 1 pound bacon
- 2 (8-ounce) cans whole water chestnuts, drained
- 1½ cups ketchup
- ⅔ -1 cup sugar
- Juice of ½ lemon

Preheat oven to 350°. Cut bacon slices into thirds and wrap one piece around each water chestnut. If water chestnuts are large, cut in half. Secure bacon around chestnuts with toothpicks. Bake 30 minutes. Do not overcook. Drain fat. Make sauce by combining ketchup, sugar and lemon juice. Pour over baked bacon and water chestnuts. Bake additional 30-45 minutes.

Notes:

NOTES

soups

Soups

Beefy Bean Chowder

Black-Eyed Pea Soup

Borscht

Chicken Gumbo

Chicken Pasta Soup

Chilled Cranberry Soup

Chilled Cucumber Soup

Chilled Strawberry Soup

Corn Chowder

Cream of Pimiento Soup

Creamy Cauliflower Soup

Fish Chowder

French Onion Soup

Gazpacho

Lentil Soup

Pot Roast Soup with Fennel and Parsnips

Shrimp and Crab Bisque

Tailgate Soup

Turkey Soup with Sugar Snap Peas

Vegetable Beef Soup

Soups

Beefy Bean Chowder

Even better if made the day before serving

1 pound lean ground beef
1 tablespoon extra-virgin olive oil
1 (16-ounce) can kidney beans, rinsed and drained
1 (16-ounce) can pinto beans, rinsed and drained
1 (28-ounce) can diced tomatoes
1 quart water
1 large onion, chopped
1 bay leaf
1½ teaspoons salt
1 teaspoon thyme
½ teaspoon freshly ground black pepper
1 cup potatoes, peeled and diced
1 green bell pepper, chopped

Brown beef in oil in Dutch oven. Add kidney beans, pinto beans, tomatoes, water, onion, bay leaf, salt, thyme and black pepper. Simmer covered 1 hour. Add potatoes and bell pepper, and cook another 20 minutes. Remove bay leaf. Serves 8

Notes:

SOUPS

Black-Eyed Pea Soup

A Southern favorite

1 (16-ounce) package dried black-eyed peas
1 tablespoon extra-virgin olive oil
½ medium onion, chopped
3-4 garlic cloves, minced
1 small green bell pepper, diced
1 stalk celery, diced
6 cups water

2 (14-ounce) cans diced tomatoes
3 cups chicken broth*
1 chicken Herb-ox bouillon cube or packet
1 (4-ounce) can chopped green chilies
1 tablespoon salt, or to taste
½ teaspoon freshly ground black pepper

Cover peas with water and boil in Dutch oven 10 minutes. Remove from heat. Cover and let stand 1 hour. Drain. Remove black-eyed peas from Dutch oven.

Heat oil in Dutch oven. Add onion, garlic, bell pepper and celery, and sauté until tender. Add peas, water, tomatoes, chicken broth, bouillon, green chilies, salt and pepper. Bring to boil, reduce heat and simmer 1 hour, stirring occasionally. Serves 6 - 8

Pacific Natural Foods Chicken Broth is a gluten-free brand.

Notes:

SOUPS

Borscht

Goes well with dilled Havarti cheese and a salad

2 (16-ounce) jars sliced red beets with juice
1¼ cups beef broth*
1-2 tablespoons Lea and Perrins Worcestershire Sauce
¼ cup soy sauce**
1 garlic clove, crushed
1 large red onion, thinly sliced

1-2 large carrots, thinly sliced
1-2 tomatoes, coarsely chopped
1 teaspoon fresh dill
¼ head red cabbage, thinly sliced (optional)
Salt to taste
Garnish with sour cream

Mix all ingredients together except sour cream. Cook until beets and cabbage are tender. Serve hot or chilled. Garnish with dollop of sour cream. Serves 4 - 6

*Pacific Natural Foods Beef Broth is a gluten-free brand.
**La Choy and San-J are gluten free.

Notes:

Soups

Chicken Gumbo

This classic gumbo is rich in texture and flavor.

1 tablespoon extra-virgin olive oil
1 large sweet onion, chopped
2 carrots, peeled and chopped
2 celery stalks, chopped
1½ cups fresh okra, chopped
8 cups chicken broth*
2 cups organic chicken, cooked and chopped

4 garlic cloves, minced
½ cup cooked rice
1 cup salsa
Freshly ground black pepper to taste
½ lemon, juiced
Tabasco to taste

Heat oil in large pot over medium heat. Add onion and sauté until softened, about 5 minutes.

Add carrots, celery, okra, broth and chicken. Bring to boil and simmer 20 minutes. Add garlic and rice. Simmer 10 minutes more and add salsa, pepper, lemon juice and Tabasco. Serves 6 - 8

Pacific Natural Foods Chicken Broth is a gluten-free brand.

SOUPS

Chicken Pasta Soup

Hearty and delicious

2 tablespoons extra-virgin olive oil
1 large onion, chopped
3-4 garlic cloves, minced
1½ cups carrots, chopped
1 cup celery, chopped
1 (32-ounce) carton chicken broth*
2 chicken Herb-ox bouillon cubes or packets
2 cups water

1½ cups frozen sweet peas
3-4 cups organic chicken, cooked and chopped
4 ounces gluten-free pasta
1 teaspoon salt, or to taste
½ teaspoon freshly ground black pepper
¼ teaspoon rubbed sage

Heat oil in Dutch oven over medium heat. Add onion, garlic, carrots and celery. Sauté 10 minutes.

Add chicken broth, bouillon, water and frozen peas, and bring to boil. Add chicken, pasta, salt, pepper and sage. Reduce heat and simmer uncovered 10 minutes. Serves 6

Pacific Natural Foods Chicken Broth is a gluten-free brand.

Notes:

SOUPS

Chilled Cranberry Soup

4 cups fresh cranberries (about 1 pound)
3 cups water
1½ cups sugar
1 (3-inch) cinnamon stick
¼ teaspoon ground cloves

2 tablespoons lemon juice
1 tablespoon orange peel, finely grated
Orange peel curls (optional)
Mint leaves (optional)

Combine cranberries, water, sugar, cinnamon stick and cloves in 3-quart saucepan. Bring to boil; reduce heat. Simmer uncovered five minutes or until half of cranberries pop. Remove from heat. Stir in lemon juice and orange peel. Cool. Cover and chill 4-24 hours. Before serving, remove cinnamon stick. Top each serving with orange peel curls and mint, if desired. Serves 6 – 8

Notes:

SOUPS

Chilled Cucumber Soup

A great starter for a meal on a hot summer day

¼ cup butter
4 cups cucumbers, peeled and chopped
1 cup green onions, chopped
2 tablespoons cornstarch
¼ cup cold water

4 cups chicken broth*
Salt and freshly ground black pepper
½ cup half-and-half
Cucumber slices for garnish

Early in day:

Melt butter in large skillet over medium-high heat. Add cucumbers and green onions, and cook until onions are tender. Add chicken broth and stir well. Mix cornstarch with water until smooth, and gradually stir into soup until blended. Cook until mixture thickens slightly and begins to boil. Add salt and pepper to taste. Reduce heat to low and simmer covered 10 minutes, stirring occasionally. Refrigerate until chilled.

At serving time:

Place 2 cups of mixture in blender and blend until smooth. Strain mixture through sieve into large bowl, discarding seeds. Repeat with rest of mixture. Stir in half-and-half. Garnish with cucumber slices. Serves 5 - 6 as first course

*Pacific Natural Foods Chicken Broth is a gluten-free brand.

Notes:

Soups

Chilled Strawberry Soup

A cool, refreshing soup with a hint of lemon

3 cups fresh strawberries, washed, hulled and cut into quarters or frozen whole strawberries, thawed, drained and quartered
1⅓ cups water
⅔ cup dry white wine

1 lemon, juice and zest
⅔ cup sugar
Whole strawberries for garnish

Blend strawberries, water, wine, lemon zest, lemon juice and sugar on medium speed 10-20 seconds. Chill in freezer until soup is somewhat firm and then place in refrigerator for up to 1 hour before serving. Garnish each serving with a whole strawberry. Serves 4 - 6

Corn Chowder

2 tablespoons butter
½ cup onion, diced
½ cup celery, diced
1 tablespoon plus 1½ teaspoons rice flour
1½ cups milk

1 (14.75-ounce) can Del Monte cream-style corn
1 slice bacon, cooked crisp and crumbled
⅛ teaspoon salt
⅛ teaspoon McCormick dried mustard
Dash white pepper

Heat butter in saucepan and stir in onion and celery. Cover pan and cook until soft, 2-3 minutes. Add flour and stir constantly with wire whisk 1 minute. Gradually add milk and bring to boil. Reduce heat and cook, stirring constantly until mixture is smooth and thickened, about 2-3 minutes. Add corn, bacon, salt, mustard and pepper. Heat until warmed through. Serves 3 - 4

SOUPS

Cream of Pimiento Soup

An elegant starter for any meal

1 (4-ounce) jar diced pimiento
2 tablespoons butter
2½ tablespoons rice flour
2 cups chicken broth*

1½ cups half-and-half
2 teaspoons onion, grated
½ teaspoon salt
¼ teaspoon Tabasco

Place pimientos in food processor and blend until smooth, stopping once to scrape down sides. Melt butter in heavy saucepan over low heat; add flour and stir until smooth. Cook 1 minute. Add chicken broth and half-and-half gradually to flour mixture, and cook over medium heat. Stir constantly until mixture is thickened and bubbly. Stir in pimiento, onion, salt and Tabasco. Cook over low heat, stirring constantly, until thoroughly heated. Makes 4 cups

Pacific Natural Foods Chicken Broth is a gluten-free brand.

Notes:

Soups

Creamy Cauliflower Soup

A creamy soup without the cream

1 tablespoon butter
1 cup onion, chopped
6 cups vegetable or chicken broth*
½ cup white wine
1½ pound head of cauliflower, trimmed and chopped

⅛ teaspoon freshly ground black pepper
½ cup cooked rice
⅛ teaspoon nutmeg
Salt to taste
Optional garnishes: parsley, fresh dill or chives

Melt butter in soup pot over medium heat. Add onion and sauté until lightly golden in color. Add broth, white wine and cauliflower. Bring to boil and simmer until cauliflower is tender, about 20-25 minutes.

Add pepper, rice and nutmeg. Purée soup in food processor or blender. Add salt to taste. Serves 4 - 6

Pacific Natural Foods Chicken or Vegetable Broth is a gluten-free brand.

Notes:

SOUPS

Fish Chowder

A Boston favorite

¼ pound salt pork
6 small potatoes, peeled and sliced
2 cups fresh or frozen haddock, flaked
2 medium onions, finely minced
3 cups boiling water

2 cups milk
Dash salt
Dash pepper
1 tablespoon cornstarch
2 tablespoons cold water

Brown pork in soup pot. Remove pork and add potatoes, fish, onions and boiling water. Simmer about ½ hour or until potatoes are cooked. Add milk, salt and pepper, and cook about 5 minutes more. Combine cold water and cornstarch. Stir until blended. Add to broth and stir until thickened. Serves 4

French Onion Soup

3 tablespoons butter
1 tablespoon extra-virgin olive oil
4 cups sweet onions, sliced
1 teaspoon granulated sugar
½ teaspoon salt

2 tablespoons dry sherry
4 cups beef broth*
Freshly ground black pepper to taste
4 slices gluten-free bread**
1 cup Gruyère cheese, freshly shredded

Melt butter and oil in heavy 3-quart pot over medium heat. Cook onions, turning heat to low as they begin to brown. Simmer at least 30 minutes, stirring occasionally.

Blend in sugar and salt. Add sherry, raise heat to medium and cook, stirring constantly until all sherry has cooked off. Stir in broth, bring to boil, reduce heat and simmer 15 minutes.

Toast bread and cut into bite-sized pieces. Ladle soup into bowls, add bread pieces and sprinkle cheese on top. Serves 4

Pacific Natural Foods Beef Broth is a gluten-free brand.
**Gluten-free bread is found in the freezer section.*

SOUPS

Gazpacho

3 cups V-8 or tomato juice
3 tablespoons extra-virgin olive oil
3 large tomatoes, chopped
1 cucumber, peeled and chopped
1 medium onion, chopped

1 green bell pepper, chopped
3 garlic cloves, peeled and chopped
1 teaspoon sugar
½ teaspoon salt
½ teaspoon Tabasco

Place ⅓ of each ingredient in blender. Blend until finely chopped and transfer to large bowl. Repeat until all ingredients are blended. Mix well, cover and chill. Serves 4 – 6

Lentil Soup

2 tablespoons extra-virgin olive oil
½ cup onion, finely diced
½ cup carrot, finely diced
½ cup celery, finely diced
2 garlic cloves, minced
2 cups French green or brown lentils, sorted and rinsed
2 quarts water

2 bay leaves
1½ teaspoons salt
¼ teaspoon freshly ground black pepper
1 tablespoon Dijon mustard
1½ tablespoon fresh lemon juice
1 tablespoon red wine vinegar
Garnish: parsley leaves, and yogurt or sour cream

Heat oil in soup pot over medium-high heat. Add onion and sauté until it begins to color around edges, about 5 minutes. Add carrots, celery and garlic. Sauté 2-3 minutes and add lentils, water, bay leaves, salt and pepper. Bring to boil. Lower heat and simmer partially covered until lentils are very tender, about 1 hour.

Stir in mustard, lemon juice and red wine vinegar. Remove bay leaves. Garnish with parsley leaves and yogurt or sour cream. Serves 6

Soups

Pot Roast Soup with Fennel and Parsnips

1 tablespoon extra-virgin olive oil
1 (2-3 pound) chuck roast
4 parsnips, peeled and cut into strips
4 carrots, peeled and sliced
2 red potatoes, peeled and quartered
1 large fennel bulb, sliced
8 cups chicken broth*
1 tablespoon fresh thyme leaves

Heat oil in large soup pot over medium-high heat. Add roast and brown on both sides. Add parsnips, carrots, potatoes, fennel and broth. Cover pot and simmer 2 hours, occasionally turning roast over so it cooks evenly.

Remove chuck roast and place on cutting board. Trim away excess fat and cut meat into 2-inch chunks. Return meat to soup pot. Chill several hours or overnight. Skim off congealed fat and discard.

Before serving, reheat and add fresh thyme leaves. Serves 6

Pacific Natural Foods Chicken Broth is a gluten-free brand.

Notes:

SOUPS

Shrimp and Crab Bisque

This rich, delicate soup is an excellent first course; a small serving is more than enough!

1 pound raw shrimp in shells	2 cups half-and-half
3 cups water	1 tablespoon butter
¼ cup brandy	Salt to taste
½ cup dry white wine	Tabasco to taste
1 small yellow onion, peeled and finely chopped.	1 pound lump crabmeat*
	2 tablespoons fresh chives, minced
2 celery stalks, peeled and finely chopped	¼ teaspoon white pepper
1 medium carrot, peeled and diced	8 teaspoons dry sherry

Wash, shell and devein shrimp. Refrigerate shrimp and put shells in large saucepan with water, brandy and white wine. Bring to boil over high heat, reduce heat to low and simmer 15 minutes. Remove and discard shells. Add onions, celery and carrots to broth and continue to simmer until vegetables are tender, about 30 minutes. Add shrimp and cook until opaque, about 1 minute. Transfer to food processor and purée until smooth. Mixture may be refrigerated at this point if prepared ahead.

Pour bisque back into saucepan and cook over low heat, gradually stirring in half-and-half. Stir in butter and season to taste with salt and Tabasco sauce. Add crabmeat, reserving some for garnish, and simmer 3 minutes more. Garnish each serving with chives, crabmeat and 1 teaspoon of sherry. Makes 8 half-cup servings

Do not use imitation crabmeat. It contains gluten.

Notes:

Soups

Tailgate Soup

- 1 pound gluten-free smoked sausage, cut into 1-inch pieces
- 2 garlic cloves, minced
- 1 cup white onions, minced
- ⅓ cup green pepper, chopped
- 1 tablespoon canola oil
- 2 cups cabbage, shredded
- ½ teaspoon paprika
- 1 teaspoon marjoram
- ½ teaspoon freshly ground black pepper
- ¼ teaspoon caraway seed
- ¼ teaspoon thyme
- ¼ teaspoon red pepper flakes
- 4 cups chicken broth*
- 2 tablespoons cider vinegar
- 2 tablespoons rice flour
- 2 tablespoons water
- 1 cup sour cream

Lightly sauté smoked sausage, garlic, onion and green pepper in oil until vegetables are tender. Add cabbage and stir until cabbage starts to wilt. Stir in paprika, marjoram, black pepper, caraway seed, thyme and red pepper flakes. Cook 3 minutes. Add broth and vinegar, simmer about 20 minutes. Combine rice flour and water, and add to soup. Add sour cream and simmer until slightly thickened. Serves 6

*Pacific Natural Foods Chicken Broth is a gluten-free brand.

Notes:

SOUPS

Turkey Soup with Sugar Snap Peas

Fine with either fresh or frozen sugar snap peas

1 tablespoon extra-virgin olive oil
½ cup onions, chopped
2 packages ground turkey (about 2.5 pounds)

2 stalks celery, chopped
4 carrots, sliced
8 cups chicken broth*
8 ounces sugar snap peas

Heat oil and onions in soup pot until onions are tender, about 5 minutes. Add ground turkey. Continue to cook, stirring frequently until meat has browned.

Add celery, carrots and chicken broth. Bring to boil, reduce heat to simmer and cook 20-25 minutes. Add sugar snap peas, and cook 5 minutes longer. Serves 6 - 8

*Pacific Natural Foods Chicken Broth is a gluten-free brand.

Notes:

Soups

Vegetable Beef Soup

Great for a crowd or freezes well

3 medium onions, chopped
1½ pounds lean ground beef
2 tablespoons extra-virgin olive oil
4 cups beef broth*
6-8 garlic cloves, finely chopped
1 Herb-ox beef bouillon cube or packet
5 (14.5-ounce) cans diced tomatoes
2 cups carrots, chopped
1½ cups celery, sliced

3 cups potatoes, peeled and cubed
2 cups frozen cut green beans
1½ cups frozen nibblet corn
2-3 tablespoons parsley flakes
3 teaspoons dried basil
2 teaspoons dried thyme
1 tablespoon salt, or to taste
1 teaspoon freshly ground black pepper, or to taste

Brown onions and ground beef in oil using 12-quart soup pot. Add all remaining ingredients and simmer 1½ hours. Serves 8-10

Pacific Natural Foods Beef Broth is a gluten-free brand.

Notes:

Notes

salads

Salads

Garlic Balsamic Vinaigrette

Apple and Orange Ambrosia Salad

Artichoke and Avocado Salad with Lemon Garlic Vinaigrette

Artichoke Rice Salad

Avocado Grapefruit Spinach Salad

Bean Sprout and Mushroom Salad

Cool Rice and Cucumber Salad

Crabmeat Pasta Salad

Cranberry Salad

Cucumber Salad

Easy Spinach Salad

Emerald Isle Salad

Fresh Corn Salad

Garbanzo Bean and Cucumber Salad

Lentil Salad with Lemon Vinaigrette

Mandarin Orange Salad

Mozzarella, Tomato, Basil Salad

Oriental Slaw

Salad with Hot Bacon Dressing

South-of the-Border Salad

Strawberry and Walnut Green Salad

Tangy Summer Salad

Tropical Chicken Salad

Turkey Salad

Waldorf Salad

SALADS

Garlic Balsamic Vinaigrette

A versatile salad dressing for a variety of salads; make with white vinegar for a lighter taste.

½ teaspoon McCormick dry mustard
2 cloves garlic, pressed
¼ teaspoon salt

½ teaspoon freshly ground black pepper
2 tablespoons balsamic vinegar
6 tablespoons extra-virgin olive oil

Mix all ingredients together in container that seals well. Shake vigorously. Pour over salad and toss. Keeps well when refrigerated.

Apple and Orange Ambrosia Salad

A traditional favorite

1 (8-ounce) can crushed pineapple with juice
1 (3.5-ounce) can sweetened shredded coconut

1 (6-ounce) can orange juice concentrate
6 ounces cold water
4-5 apples (sweet/tart apples like Macintosh work well)

Mix together well pineapple, coconut, orange juice and water in medium-sized bowl. Work with apples one or two at a time. Peel, core and grate, putting them immediately into juice mixture. Stir well. This will prevent them from turning brown.

When apples have been grated and blended into juice mixture, cover bowl with plastic wrap and refrigerate so apples have time to absorb juice. Ambrosia salad can sit overnight before serving. It also will keep several days. Serves 6 - 8

Notes:

SALADS

Artichoke and Avocado Salad with Lemon Garlic Vinaigrette

1 (10-ounce) bag salad greens
1 (14-ounce) can artichoke hearts, drained
1 ripe avocado, peeled and sliced
1 ripe tomato, peeled and sliced
1 slice red onion cut in half

Open bag of salad greens, wash at least twice and drain. Place greens in bowl and add artichoke hearts, avocado, tomato and red onion.

Lemon Garlic Vinaigrette:

1 large garlic clove, minced
½ teaspoon salt
3 tablespoons fresh lemon juice
5 tablespoons extra-virgin olive oil

Place garlic and salt in small bowl and mash into paste with back of spoon. Add lemon juice and oil. Blend well.

Toss salad with dressing. Serves 4 – 6

Notes:

SALADS

Artichoke Rice Salad

This recipe can easily be doubled or tripled for a crowd. Great for an elegant dinner or a picnic

3 cups rice
1 large (10-grams) Knorr vegetarian vegetable bouillon cube*
2 (7-ounce) jars marinated artichoke hearts, quartered
⅓ cup green pepper, finely chopped
½ cup green onions, finely chopped
⅓ cup green olives, sliced
½ cup mayonnaise**
1½ teaspoons McCormick curry
Freshly ground black pepper to taste

Prepare rice according to package directions, dissolving bouillon cube in boiling water before adding rice. Let rice cool 15 minutes. Drain artichokes, reserving liquid. Add artichokes, green pepper, onions and olives to rice. Whisk together in small bowl mayonnaise, ¼ cup marinade from artichokes and curry powder. Toss rice mixture and dressing together with pepper. If mixture is too dry, add small amount extra mayonnaise, but do not add more artichoke marinade. Chill. Serves 6

*Knorr Vegetarian Vegetable Bouillon has flavoring important to the salad.
**Kraft and Hellmann's are gluten free.

Avocado Grapefruit Spinach Salad

1 bunch or 1 (12-ounce) package fresh spinach
2 tablespoons fresh lemon juice
1 ripe avocado, peeled and thinly sliced
1 red grapefruit, peeled and sectioned
1 red onion, sliced
Gluten-free salad dressing of choice

Wash, drain and tear spinach into bite-sized pieces and place in bowl. Pour lemon juice over avocado to prevent browning. Put avocado, grapefruit and onion on spinach, add dressing, and toss. Serves 4 - 6

SALADS

Bean Sprout and Mushroom Salad

⅓ cup extra-virgin olive oil
¼ cup white wine
2 tablespoons sesame seeds, toasted
½ teaspoon salt
½ teaspoon McCormick dry mustard

½ teaspoon McCormick garlic powder
4 ounces fresh mushrooms, sliced
4 cups lettuce, shredded
8 ounces fresh bean sprouts or 1 (16-ounce) can bean sprouts, drained

Combine oil, wine, sesame seeds, salt, mustard and garlic for dressing. Mix well and chill. Just before serving, toss mushrooms, lettuce and bean sprouts with dressing. Serves 6 - 8

Cool Rice and Cucumber Salad

1½ cups long-grain white rice
3 cups water
1¼ teaspoons salt, divided
2 cucumbers, peeled, seeded and finely chopped
½ cup fresh parsley, finely chopped

3 tablespoons fresh dill, chopped
¼ cup green onions, white and green parts, chopped
¼ cup white wine vinegar
3 tablespoons extra-virgin olive oil
½ cup plain yogurt

Rinse rice in strainer and drain. Bring 3 cups water to boil in medium saucepan. Add 1 teaspoon salt and rice to boiling water. Return to boil, lower heat, cover and simmer until tender, about 18-20 minutes.

While rice is cooking, place cucumbers, parsley and dill in large bowl and set aside.

Combine green onions, vinegar, oil and ¼ teaspoon salt in small bowl.

After rice has finished cooking, cool briefly and add to cucumbers and herbs. Add green onion mixture and yogurt, and toss gently. Taste and adjust seasoning. Serves 6

SALADS

Crabmeat Pasta Salad

Colorful and delicious

8 ounces gluten-free pasta
2 tablespoons butter
⅓ cup onion, minced
1 large carrot, shredded
1 garlic clove, minced
1 teaspoon dried basil

2 tablespoons dried parsley
¼ cup extra-virgin olive oil
12 ounces fresh crabmeat*
1 tablespoon lemon juice
½ teaspoon salt

Cook pasta according to directions. Drain, add butter and toss. In large skillet, sauté onion, carrot, garlic, basil and parsley in oil until vegetables are tender. Add crabmeat, lemon juice and salt. Simmer 8-10 minutes. Stir once or twice. Toss with pasta and chill. Serves 4

Do not use imitation crabmeat. It contains gluten.

Cranberry Salad

A tasty accompaniment with Thanksgiving dinner

4 cups fresh cranberries
2 cups sugar
2 (3-ounce) packages lemon Jell-O
1½ cups hot water

1 orange, quartered and seeded
1 cup crushed pineapple, drained
½ cup walnuts, chopped
1 cup celery, chopped

Grind cranberries in food processor and place in bowl with sugar. Let stand 3-4 hours or overnight in refrigerator. The next day, mix Jell-O with hot water. Grind up orange including rind in food processor. Mix with Jell-O, pineapple, walnuts and celery, and add cranberry mixture. Put in refrigerator until set. Serves 8-10

SALADS

Cucumber Salad

Will keep for up to a week in the refrigerator

6 medium cucumbers, peeled and thinly sliced
3 garlic cloves, minced
Salt to taste

3 tablespoons white vinegar
⅓ cup sugar
Paprika (optional)
Freshly ground black pepper (optional)

Toss cucumber slices with garlic and salt, coating well. Cover and allow to stand at room temperature 45-60 minutes, stirring occasionally. Pour into colander and press to squeeze out as much water as possible.

Stir vinegar and sugar in small bowl until sugar dissolves. The mixture should be thick, not too watery.

Combine cucumbers and vinegar/sugar mixture. Store in glass jar in refrigerator. If desired, sprinkle with paprika and black pepper when serving. Serves 8

Notes:

SALADS

Easy Spinach Salad

12 ounces fresh spinach
2 tablespoons butter
1 garlic clove, pressed

1 cup walnut pieces
1 orange, peeled and sliced

Tear spinach into pieces and chill. Combine butter and garlic over medium heat; add walnuts and brown, stirring continuously. Drain walnuts. Toss orange slices and walnuts with spinach.

Dressing: (Makes 1¾ cups)

⅓ cup granulated sugar
1 teaspoon salt
1 teaspoon paprika
¼ cup orange juice

2½ tablespoons lemon juice
1 tablespoon cider vinegar
1 tablespoon onion, finely chopped
1 cup extra-virgin olive oil

To make dressing, combine ingredients in jar and shake well. Use enough dressing to lightly cover salad. Serves 6 - 8

Emerald Isle Salad

2 cups water
1 (3-ounce) package lemon Jell-O
1 (3-ounce) package lime Jell-O
1 (8-ounce) package cream cheese

1 (16-ounce) can crushed pineapple, with juice
1 (8-ounce) carton Cool Whip

Boil water in large saucepan and remove from heat. Immediately add both packages Jell-O to hot water, stirring constantly until dissolved.

Cut cream cheese into chunks and blend with Jell-O mixture, stirring gently to avoid creating foam. Add crushed pineapple with juice. Chill a few minutes until salad begins to congeal, but has not completely set. Remove from refrigerator.

Fold in Cool Whip and pour mixture into 9 x 13-inch pan. Refrigerate again several hours to allow salad to set. Serves 8 -10

SALADS

Fresh Corn Salad

A colorful summer salad

3 cups fresh corn (about 5 ears)
½ cup red onions, chopped
3 tablespoons cider vinegar
3 tablespoons extra-virgin olive oil

½ teaspoon kosher salt
½ teaspoon freshly ground black pepper
½ cup fresh basil leaves, chopped
Dash Tabasco (optional)

Cook corn in boiling, salted water 3 minutes; drain. Cool corn. Cut kernels from cob using sharp knife.

Combine corn, red onions, vinegar, oil, salt and pepper in serving bowl. Just before serving, stir in basil. Season to taste with additional salt, pepper and Tabasco. Serves 4 – 6

Garbanzo Bean and Cucumber Salad

1 (15-ounce) can garbanzo beans, rinsed
  and drained
½ cup red bell pepper, finely chopped
1 small red onion, finely chopped
1 medium cucumber, finely chopped
1 tablespoon balsamic vinegar

3 tablespoons extra-virgin olive oil
1 garlic clove, pressed
½ teaspoon dried oregano
¼ teaspoon salt
½ teaspoon freshly ground black pepper

Toss all ingredients together. Chill. Keeps well when refrigerated. Serves 4

Notes:

SALADS

Lentil Salad with Lemon Vinaigrette

2 cups lentils, rinsed and drained
¼ teaspoon kosher salt

2 bay leaves
2½ quarts water

Place lentils, salt, bay leaves and water in pot. Cover and simmer 30 minutes. Lentils should be soft, but not mushy. Drain.

Lemon Vinaigrette:

1 garlic clove, pressed
½ teaspoon salt
4 strips lemon peel
1 tablespoon wine vinegar

1 tablespoon lemon juice
2 drops Tabasco
1 tablespoon Dijon mustard
½ cup extra-virgin olive oil

Mix garlic, salt and lemon peel. Add vinegar, lemon juice, Tabasco, mustard and oil. Blend well. Add vinaigrette mixture to warm lentils. Can be served hot or cold. Serves 6

Notes:

SALADS

Mandarin Orange Salad

A light accompaniment to any meal

¼ cup slivered almonds
1 (10-ounce) bag chopped lettuce, washed
¾ cup celery, chopped

1 (11-ounce) can mandarin oranges, drained
¼ cup red onion, sliced

Preheat oven to 350°. Place almonds in small baking pan and toast until lightly browned, about 5 minutes. Remove immediately and cool.

Combine lettuce, celery, oranges and onion in large salad bowl. Just before serving, add toasted almonds.

Dressing:

¼ cup extra-virgin olive oil
2 tablespoons sugar

½ teaspoon salt
2 tablespoons red wine vinegar

Place oil, sugar, salt and red wine vinegar in small container with lid. Shake well. Dress salad and toss. Serve immediately. Serves 4

Notes:

SALADS

Mozzarella, Tomato, Basil Salad

Great summer salad using fresh ingredients

4 tablespoons extra-virgin olive oil
1 large garlic clove, pressed
Salt and freshly ground black pepper to taste
2 tablespoons fresh lemon juice

¼ pound mozzarella cheese
3 large ripe tomatoes, quartered and thinly sliced
2 cups fresh basil leaves

Combine oil, garlic, salt, pepper and lemon juice in small bowl. Slice mozzarella into thin pieces, approximately the same size as tomato slices. Season tomato slices lightly with salt and pepper, and add cheese.

Drizzle half of dressing over tomato-cheese mixture and reserve other half until serving. Wash and dry basil leaves. If leaves are small, leave whole or if large, chop coarsely.

Toss basil leaves and remaining dressing with tomato-cheese mixture just before serving. Serves 6 - 8

Notes:

SALADS

Oriental Slaw

This slaw has a surprising kick!

Dressing:

3 tablespoons sugar
2 tablespoons red wine vinegar
2 tablespoons soy sauce*
½ cup extra-virgin olive oil
½ teaspoon salt

½ teaspoon freshly ground black pepper
Dash Tabasco
½ teaspoon chives
½ teaspoon McCormick garlic powder

Combine all dressing ingredients, mix well and set aside.

Slaw:

2 (10-ounce) bags shredded coleslaw
6 green onions, finely chopped
1-2 jalapeño peppers, seeded and finely chopped

5-6 radishes, cut into match sticks
3 tablespoons salted sunflower seeds
½ cup slivered or sliced almonds, toasted

Toss coleslaw, onions, jalapeños and radishes in large bowl. Pour dressing over salad and mix well. Before serving add sunflower seeds and almonds. Toss to mix well. Serves 8

*La Choy and San-J are gluten free.

Notes:

SALADS

Salad with Hot Bacon Dressing

1 head of romaine lettuce, broken into bite-sized pieces

½ cup green onion, thinly sliced
6 slices bacon

Dressing:

2 tablespoons granulated sugar
3 tablespoons cider vinegar
1 egg, well beaten

3 tablespoons reserved bacon drippings
Salt and pepper to taste

Wash lettuce leaves and pat dry. Place lettuce and onion in bowl, cover and chill. Fry bacon until crisp, drain, reserving 3 tablespoons fat. Crumble bacon. Gradually mix sugar, vinegar and egg with bacon drippings. Cook over medium-low heat, stirring until thickened. Do not boil. Remove from heat, pour over lettuce and onions. Add crumbled bacon, salt and pepper. Serve immediately. Serves 6 - 8

South-of-the-Border Salad

Hearty enough for a meal

1 tablespoon extra-virgin olive oil
1 pound lean ground beef
Salt and pepper to taste
1 head lettuce, shredded
1 medium onion, chopped
4 tomatoes, diced
4 ounces cheddar cheese, freshly grated

1 (8-ounce) bottle gluten-free French dressing
Dash Tabasco
1 (16-ounce) can red kidney beans, drained
1 medium bag gluten-free tortilla chips, crushed
Gluten-free taco sauce

Heat oil in skillet over medium-high heat. Add ground beef and brown. Drain beef; add salt and pepper. Mix beef, lettuce, onions, tomatoes, cheese, dressing, Tabasco, beans and chips in large bowl. Serve with taco sauce. Serves 6 - 8

Salads

Strawberry and Walnut Green Salad

16 strawberries, washed and sliced in half
½ cup whole walnuts, lightly toasted

1 (10-ounce) bag mixed greens
1 slice red onion, cut in half

Place strawberries in salad bowl and add walnuts. Add greens and red onion to bowl.

Dressing:

¼ cup extra-virgin olive oil
2 tablespoons sugar

½ teaspoon salt
2 tablespoons red wine vinegar

Place oil, sugar, salt and vinegar in small container with lid. Shake well.

Dress salad and toss just before serving. Serves 4

Notes:

SALADS

Tangy Summer Salad

Great with fresh vegetables from the garden

8 large firm, ripe tomatoes, peeled
1 large green pepper, cut into thin strips
1 red onion, sliced into thin rings

1 cucumber, peeled and sliced just before serving

Dressing:

¾ cup cider vinegar
1½ teaspoons celery salt
1½ teaspoons mustard seed
½ teaspoon freshly ground black pepper

½ teaspoon salt
4½ teaspoons granulated sugar
⅛ teaspoon red pepper or more to taste
¼ cup cold water

Cut each tomato into bite-sized pieces. Place tomatoes, green pepper and onions in bowl. Heat vinegar, celery salt, mustard seed, pepper, salt, sugar, red pepper and water. Boil on high 1 minute. While hot, pour over tomato mixture. Chill. Stir occasionally. Add cucumbers just before serving. The dressing will keep 3-4 days in refrigerator. Serves 8

Notes:

SALADS

Tropical Chicken Salad

Hearty enough for a main course

4 cups organic chicken, cooked and diced
1 cup celery, chopped
1 cup grapes, halved
1 cup sliced almonds, toasted
4 slices bacon, cooked, drained and crumbled
1 apple, cored and cubed
1 (8-ounce) can pineapple tidbits, drained
1 (11-ounce) can mandarin oranges, drained
Whole lettuce leaves

Combine chicken, celery, grapes, almonds, bacon, apple, pineapple and mandarin oranges in large bowl.

Dressing:

1 cup mayonnaise*
1 cup sour cream
1 teaspoon salt
2 tablespoons lemon juice

Combine dressing ingredients in small bowl and add to chicken mixture. Toss lightly. Chill thoroughly and serve on whole lettuce leaves. Serves 8 - 10

Kraft and Hellmann's are gluten free.

Turkey Salad

3-4 cups cooked organic turkey breast, chopped
1½ cups celery, chopped
2 cups seedless grapes, halved
1 cup mayonnaise*
Lettuce leaves

Mix all ingredients and refrigerate, except lettuce. Serve on lettuce leaves. Serves 5 - 6

Kraft and Hellmann's are gluten free.

Salads

Waldorf Salad

¼ cup walnuts, chopped
1 stalk celery, chopped
2 apples, peeled, cored and cut into bite-sized pieces

¼ cup raisins
2-3 tablespoons mayonnaise*

Preheat oven to 350°. Toast walnuts on cookie sheet until lightly browned, 6-9 minutes. Cool briefly.

Place walnuts, celery, apples and raisins in bowl. Add 2 tablespoons mayonnaise. Stir well. If not coated, add more mayonnaise. Chill until ready to serve. Serves 4

Kraft and Hellmann's are gluten free.

Notes:

Notes

sides

Sides

- Gluten-Free Bread Crumbs
- Asparagus with Shiitake Mushrooms and Tarragon
- Baked Beans
- Basmati Rice with Garlic
- Butternut Squash, Cauliflower and Bok Choy
- Cauliflower and Broccoli Sauté
- Cheesy Potatoes
- Chinese Sesame Pasta
- Creamy Horseradish Potatoes
- Creamy Sweet Potatoes
- Curried Fruit
- Dressing with Roasted Garlic and Apples
- Garlic Mashed Potatoes
- German Sauerkraut
- Greek Potato Salad
- Italian Green Beans
- Mashed Potatoes Parmesan
- Nutty Brussels Sprouts
- Old-Fashioned Potato Salad
- Orange Honey-Glazed Carrots
- Oven-Roasted Broccoli and Cauliflower
- Oven-Roasted Sweet Potatoes
- Peppers and Onion Sauté
- Red Cabbage
- Roasted Asparagus with Parmesan
- Roasted Potatoes with Garlic and Thyme
- Sautéed Green Beans and Onions
- Savory Zucchini with Bacon
- Scalloped Corn
- Simple Yellow Squash
- Spinach with Raisins and Pine Nuts
- Steamed Butternut Squash and Fennel
- Sweet and Sour Cabbage
- Sweet Potato Risotto
- Sweet Potatoes with Orange Glaze
- White Rice with Mushrooms
- White Rice with Peas
- Zucchini and Sweet Onion Sauté

SIDES

Gluten-Free Bread Crumbs

8 slices gluten-free bread*

Preheat oven to 325º. Place bread slices on cookie sheet and bake about 15 minutes. If bread is frozen, it will take longer. Bake until bread is quite dry but not overly toasted. Remove and cool on rack.

Cut or tear bread into chunks and place in food processor. Process until all pieces are broken down into bread crumbs. Eight slices of bread should yield about 2 cups bread crumbs. To make very fine bread crumbs, process crumbs again.

*Gluten-free bread is found in the freezer section.

Asparagus with Shiitake Mushrooms and Tarragon

1 pound fresh asparagus	½ cup water
1 (4-ounce) package shiitake mushrooms	2 tablespoons soy sauce*
1½ tablespoons butter, divided	½ teaspoon dried tarragon

Cut asparagus stalks on diagonal, discarding white ends. Remove stems from mushrooms and slice tops.

Melt 1 tablespoon butter in large skillet over medium-high heat. Add mushrooms, sauté 3-4 minutes, remove from skillet and set aside.

Add asparagus pieces and water to skillet. Cover and allow asparagus to cook five minutes, stirring occasionally. Remove cover. Stir in soy sauce, tarragon and remaining ½ tablespoon butter. Continue to cook until most of water has evaporated, about 5 minutes. Return mushrooms to skillet and stir well. Remove skillet from heat and serve. Serves 4

*La Choy and San-J are gluten free.

SIDES

Baked Beans

Good accompaniment for hamburgers and hot dogs

2 (16-ounce) cans Bush's Best Baked Beans
½ cup brown sugar
1 teaspoon McCormick dry mustard
½ cup ketchup
½ cup onion, diced
4 slices bacon (optional)

Preheat oven to 350°. Mix beans, sugar, mustard, ketchup and onions, and place in casserole dish. If desired, lay slices of bacon on top. Bake 1 hour. Serves 6 - 8

Basmati Rice with Garlic

2 cups basmati rice
4 cups water
1 teaspoon salt
2 garlic cloves, minced
1 tablespoon extra-virgin olive oil

Place rice in strainer, rinse under cold water and drain. Put water, salt, garlic and oil in large saucepan with lid. Heat to boiling and add rice. Cover saucepan, turn heat to low and cook 18-20 minutes. Remove from burner and let sit covered 10 minutes to allow rice to steam. Serves 6 - 8

Notes:

SIDES

Butternut Squash, Cauliflower and Bok Choy

A medley of vegetables especially good with pork and chicken

1 small butternut squash, peeled and seeded
½ head cauliflower, separated into florets
1 head bok choy or 3 heads baby bok choy, trimmed and chopped
1-2 tablespoons butter
Salt and pepper to taste

Cut butternut squash into 2-inch squares. Place steamer basket over boiling pot water. Add squash and cauliflower, cover pot and steam until vegetables are just tender when poked with knife, about 15 minutes. Add bok choy and continue steaming 3-4 more minutes.

Place vegetables in warm bowl. Cut butter into pieces and add to vegetables. Wait 2 minutes for butter to melt, and add salt and pepper. Gently toss and serve. Serves 6

Cauliflower and Broccoli Sauté

1 head cauliflower, cut into florets
Boiling, salted water
1 bunch broccoli, cut into florets
½ cup butter
2-4 garlic cloves, minced
1½ -2 cups mushrooms, sliced
2 Herb-ox chicken bouillon cubes or packets
3-5 tablespoons soy sauce*
Salt and pepper to taste

Cook cauliflower in water until tender-crisp, about 5 minutes. Remove from pot with slotted spoon and set aside. Add more water to pot if needed. Add broccoli to pot and cook until tender-crisp and bright green. Drain and add broccoli with cauliflower. Melt butter in pot over medium-low heat and sauté garlic until lightly golden. Add mushrooms and sauté until tender. Stir in bouillon and mix well. Add cauliflower, broccoli and soy sauce, and stir-fry 5 minutes. Season with salt and pepper. Serves 8

*La Choy and San-J are gluten free.

SIDES

Cheesy Potatoes

Must be prepared a day ahead

8-10 medium potatoes
½ pint heavy cream
1 cup milk
½ teaspoon salt

1 teaspoon McCormick dry mustard
8 ounces fresh sharp cheddar cheese, cubed
Dash nutmeg

Cook, cool and peel potatoes. Grate potatoes into buttered 9 x 13-inch pan. Heat cream, milk, salt, mustard, cheese and nutmeg until cheese melts. Pour mixture over potatoes. Place in refrigerator 24 hours. Preheat oven to 350°. Bake 30 minutes. Serves 6

Chinese Sesame Pasta

This recipe is best if made the day before serving.

2 tablespoons soy sauce*
1½ teaspoons rice wine vinegar
1 teaspoon sesame oil
1 tablespoon canola oil

2 garlic cloves, pressed
2 green onions including green tops, minced
8 ounces gluten-free pasta

Mix all ingredients except pasta. Prepare pasta according to package directions and toss with sauce. Serve warm or chilled. Serves 4 - 6

*La Choy and San-J are gluten free.

Notes:

SIDES

Creamy Horseradish Potatoes

May be prepared ahead, refrigerated and baked before serving.

3½ pounds red potatoes, unpeeled
1 tablespoon salt
1½-2 cups milk
½ cup unsalted butter

½ cup sour cream
2-4 tablespoons prepared horseradish*
1 teaspoon salt, or to taste
½ teaspoon freshly ground black pepper

Cover potatoes with water in 6-quart pot, add salt and bring to boil. Simmer, covered, until potatoes are tender, 30-35 minutes. Drain potatoes and return to pot. Heat milk and butter in small saucepan. Mash hot potatoes in pot. Gradually add hot milk and butter, and mash again until well blended. Fold in sour cream, horseradish, salt and pepper. Serve immediately, or transfer to casserole dish and refrigerate. To reheat, bake uncovered 20-30 minutes at 400°. Serves 6

* Be sure to read label on horseradish – some contain gluten!

Notes:

Sides

Creamy Sweet Potatoes

3 cups sweet potatoes, cooked and mashed
⅓ cup sugar
2 eggs, well-beaten
1 teaspoon vanilla extract
1 tablespoon orange zest
¼ cup butter
½ cup heavy cream

Mix all ingredients together and place in buttered baking dish.

Topping:

⅓ cup brown sugar
½ cup rice flour
1 tablespoon orange zest
1 cup pecans, chopped
¼ cup butter

Preheat oven to 350°. Mix topping ingredients together and sprinkle over sweet potatoes. Bake 30 minutes. May be prepared ahead and refrigerated. Bring dish to room temperature before baking. Serves 6 - 8

Curried Fruit

Good side with pork or ham; best prepared the day before

1 (16-ounce) can pear halves or pieces
1 (16-ounce) can sliced cling peaches
1 (16-ounce) can pineapple chunks or spears
1 (16-ounce) can apricot halves
12 maraschino cherries, cut in half (optional)
⅔ cup slivered almonds
¾ cup light brown sugar
1-3 teaspoons McCormick curry powder, according to taste
⅓ cup butter, melted

Preheat oven to 325°. Drain all fruit and place in 2½-quart casserole. Sprinkle with almonds. Combine sugar, curry powder and melted butter in small bowl. Pour mixture over fruit and nuts. Cover and bake 1 hour. Serve or refrigerate for later serving. If made ahead, reheat 30 minutes at 350°. Serves 8 - 10

Sides

Dressing with Roasted Garlic and Apples

Make ahead, refrigerate and warm in 350° oven before serving.

1 bulb fresh garlic, unpeeled
1 tablespoon butter
1 tablespoon extra-virgin olive oil
1 cup onions, minced
1 cup celery, finely chopped
¼ cup shallots
1 cup Granny Smith apples, peeled, cored and diced
2 cups gluten-free chicken broth*
4 cups gluten-free bread, toasted and cut into cubes**
¼ cup parsley, finely chopped
⅛ teaspoon nutmeg
½ teaspoon dried sage
Salt and pepper to taste

Preheat oven to 375°. Place unpeeled garlic bulb in small ovenproof pan with ¼-inch water. Roast garlic about 30 minutes or until garlic cloves have softened and can be easily squeezed from bulb. Squeeze garlic into small bowl and mash.

Heat butter and oil in large skillet, and sauté onions, celery, shallots and apples, about 5 minutes. Add 2 cups chicken broth and simmer until liquid is reduced by half. Add bread cubes, garlic purée, parsley, nutmeg, sage, salt and pepper. Stir well and serve. Serves 8

*Pacific Natural Foods Chicken Broth is a gluten-free brand.
**Gluten-free bread is found in the freezer section.

Garlic Mashed Potatoes

3 pounds potatoes, peeled and diced
1 teaspoon salt
3 large garlic cloves, minced
4 tablespoons butter
½ cup whipping cream
1 cup milk

Place potatoes in pot with enough water to cover. Add salt and garlic. Boil potatoes until tender. Drain potatoes, reserving one cup liquid. Mash potatoes with butter. Add cream and milk. Continue mashing until smooth, using as much reserved liquid as needed to reach desired consistency. Serve immediately. Serves 4

SIDES

German Sauerkraut

Make a day ahead to enhance flavor.

4-5 (14.5-ounce) cans sauerkraut
4 tablespoons butter
1 large onion, minced
2 medium apples, peeled, cored and chopped

2 cups beef broth*
1 tablespoon caraway seeds
1 large raw potato, peeled and grated
Salt, optional

Drain sauerkraut, rinse well, press out excess water and set aside. Melt butter in Dutch oven. Add onions and apples, reduce heat and sauté slowly until golden brown. Add sauerkraut and stir well. Cover and cook slowly over very low heat, 10 minutes. Add enough broth to half-cover sauerkraut. Add caraway seeds. Cover and simmer slowly 1½ hours. Stir occasionally and add more broth to pot, if needed. Add grated potato, stir well and continue simmering another 20-30 minutes. Season with salt, if desired. Serves 8

Pacific Natural Foods Beef Broth is a gluten-free brand.

Notes:

SIDES

Greek Potato Salad

A tasty alternative to traditional potato salad

7 medium red potatoes, unpeeled
½ cup green onion, chopped
1 green pepper, sliced into thin strips

8 ounces feta cheese, cut into small pieces
Pitted black olives (optional)
Mint leaves, chopped (optional)

Boil potatoes until soft, but not mushy. Cut into small cubes. Toss potatoes with onion, green pepper, and feta in large bowl.

Dressing:

½ teaspoon garlic powder
2 teaspoons prepared Dijon mustard
¾ cup extra-virgin olive oil

⅓ cup white vinegar
½ teaspoon dried oregano

In separate bowl blend together dressing ingredients. Pour over warm potato mixture and toss. Chill. Before serving, add black olives and mint, if desired. Serves 8 - 10

Italian Green Beans

When fresh vegetables are not available, try this easy recipe.

1 large sweet onion, chopped
4-6 garlic cloves, minced
2 tablespoons extra-virgin olive oil
2 (14.5-ounce) cans green beans, drained

1 (14.5-ounce) can diced tomatoes
½ teaspoon oregano
½ teaspoon basil

Sauté onions and garlic in oil over medium heat 10 minutes. Add green beans, tomatoes, oregano and basil. Stir and sauté 5 minutes longer. Serves 5 - 6

SIDES

Mashed Potatoes Parmesan

Make ahead, refrigerate and bake just before serving

3½ pounds red potatoes, unpeeled
1 tablespoon salt
1½-2 cups milk
½ cup unsalted butter
½ cup sour cream
½ cup freshly grated Parmesan cheese
1 teaspoons salt, or to taste
½ teaspoon freshly ground black pepper

Cover potatoes and salt with water in 6-quart pot and bring to boil. Simmer covered until potatoes are tender, 30-35 minutes. Drain potatoes and return to pot. Heat milk and butter in small saucepan. Mash hot potatoes in pot. Gradually add hot milk and butter, and mash again until well blended. Fold in sour cream, cheese, salt and pepper. Serve immediately or transfer to casserole dish and refrigerate. To reheat, bake uncovered 20-30 minutes at 400°. Serves 6

Nutty Brussels Sprouts

Unique nutty flavor complements any meat

1 tablespoon extra-virgin olive oil
1 medium onion, chopped
4-6 garlic cloves, minced
2 pounds Brussels sprouts, halved and thinly sliced
½ cup chicken broth*
1 tablespoon sugar
½ teaspoon salt
¼ cup pecans, toasted and chopped

Heat oil in large non-stick skillet over medium heat. Sauté onions 5 minutes. Add garlic and sauté 5 minutes longer. Raise heat to medium-high; add Brussels sprouts and sauté 5 minutes. Add broth, sugar and salt. Cook until liquid evaporates, about 5 minutes more. Stir frequently. Remove to serving dish and sprinkle with pecans. Serves 4 - 6

Pacific Natural Foods Chicken Broth is a gluten-free brand.

SIDES

Old-Fashioned Potato Salad

6 medium potatoes, peeled
1 small onion, finely chopped
1 teaspoon salt
⅛ teaspoon freshly ground black pepper

¼ cup gluten-free Italian salad dressing
½ cup mayonnaise*
½ cup celery, chopped
2 hard boiled eggs, chopped

Boil potatoes in water until done, but still firm. Cool. Cut into cubes and combine with onions. Sprinkle with salt and pepper, and mix with Italian dressing. Cover and refrigerate at least 2 hours before serving. Just before serving, add mayonnaise and mix well. Stir in celery and eggs. Serves 6

Kraft and Hellmann's are gluten free.

Orange Honey-Glazed Carrots

2 cups baby carrots, sliced in half lengthwise
3 tablespoons honey
1 tablespoon butter

¼ teaspoon salt
⅓ cup orange juice
⅛ teaspoon ground cloves

Place carrots in steamer and cook until slightly soft, but not mushy, or boil carrots in small saucepan and drain.

In separate saucepan, add honey and butter, and cook on low heat until honey starts to bubble. Add salt, orange juice and cloves, stir and add steamed carrots. Serves 4

Notes:

Sides

Oven-Roasted Broccoli and Cauliflower

1 bunch broccoli, cut into florets
1 head cauliflower, cut into florets
1 large onion, coarsely chopped
3 tablespoons extra-virgin olive oil
4 garlic cloves, minced

1 teaspoon salt
½ teaspoon freshly ground black pepper
1 tablespoon rosemary
¼ cup Parmesan cheese, freshly grated

Preheat oven to 400°. Place broccoli, cauliflower, onion, oil, garlic, salt, pepper and rosemary in roasting pan, and toss until well coated. Roast 30 minutes, stirring once after 15 minutes. Sprinkle with cheese and serve. Serves 6 - 8

Oven-Roasted Sweet Potatoes

Simple, healthy, delicious

Sweet potatoes, peeled and sliced into
   ½ -inch slices

Extra-virgin olive oil

Preheat oven to 400°. Place sweet potato slices on baking sheet and brush with oil. Bake 20 minutes.

Notes:

SIDES

Peppers and Onion Sauté

Great as a topping for sandwiches, or add chunks of kielbasa and serve over rice.

1 large onion, halved and thinly sliced
2 tablespoons extra-virgin olive oil
5-6 green, red and yellow bell peppers, coarsely chopped
½ teaspoon salt
¼ teaspoon McCormick garlic powder
¼ teaspoon Italian seasoning
¼ teaspoon freshly ground black pepper
2 tomatoes, chopped

Sauté onions in oil until tender. Add peppers, and sprinkle with salt, garlic powder, Italian seasoning and pepper. Continue sautéing until peppers are tender. Add tomatoes and heat through. **Do not cover and do not over cook.** Serves 4

Notes:

SIDES

Red Cabbage

A colorful side dish with beef or pork

1 (2-3 pound) head red cabbage	Salt
2-3 tablespoons butter	1-2 cups beef broth*, as needed
1 tablespoon sugar	1 tablespoon cornstarch
1 large apple, peeled, cored and chopped	¼ cup cold water
1 medium onion, minced	¼ teaspoon ground cloves
¼ cup white or wine vinegar	¼ teaspoon allspice

Shred cabbage, discarding core and tough ribs. Heat butter in Dutch oven. Add sugar to hot butter and sauté slowly until golden brown. Add apples and onions; cover and cook mixture over very low heat 3-4 minutes.

Add shredded cabbage and toss to coat with butter. Pour vinegar over cabbage and stir to mix thoroughly. Cover pot and cook over low heat about 10 minutes, or until cabbage has turned bright purple. Cooking slowly is very important. Otherwise, cabbage will be a faded pink.

Sprinkle with salt, add 1 cup broth, cover and simmer slowly 1½-2 hours, until cabbage is tender. Add more broth, if needed, as cabbage cooks. Mix cornstarch and water in small bowl, and add to hot but not boiling cabbage, stirring well. Season with cloves and allspice. Serves 4 - 6

Pacific Natural Foods Beef Broth is a gluten-free brand.

Notes:

SIDES

Roasted Asparagus with Parmesan

A healthy way to cook asparagus

2 pounds fresh asparagus
Extra-virgin olive oil
Garlic salt

¼ cup lemon juice
½ cup Parmesan cheese, freshly grated

Preheat oven to 400°. Snap off tough ends of asparagus. Place on cookie sheet, brush with olive oil and sprinkle lightly with garlic salt. Bake 15 minutes. Transfer to serving platter, and sprinkle with lemon juice and cheese. Serves 4 - 6

Roasted Potatoes with Garlic and Thyme

2-3 tablespoons salt
2 cups water
1½ pounds Yukon Gold or Red potatoes, peeled and quartered

1 bulb fresh garlic cloves, separated but unpeeled
2 tablespoons extra-virgin olive oil
1 teaspoon dried thyme
Salt and pepper to taste

Preheat oven to 425°. Place salt in bowl, add cold water and stir until dissolved. Add potatoes to salted water. Add more water to cover potatoes if needed. Set aside 15 minutes.

Lightly oil baking dish. Remove potatoes from salted water and dry with paper towels. Toss potatoes with unpeeled garlic cloves, oil, thyme, salt and pepper in bowl. Place in baking dish and bake uncovered 30-45 minutes until potatoes are tender and browned around edges. Serves 4

Notes:

SIDES

Sautéed Green Beans and Onions

1 tablespoon extra-virgin olive oil
1 medium onion, chopped

2 (14.5-ounce) cans green beans, drained
1 teaspoon Italian seasoning

Heat oil in large skillet. Sauté onions over medium-low heat 10 minutes. Add green beans and seasoning, mix well and continue to sauté 5-10 minutes. Serves 4 - 6

Savory Zucchini with Bacon

3 slices bacon, chopped
1 medium onion, chopped
3-4 medium zucchini, sliced

1 (8-ounce) can tomato sauce
½ teaspoon salt
¼ teaspoon freshly ground black pepper

Partially fry bacon. Add onion and cook until golden. Add zucchini, tomato sauce, salt and pepper. Cover and cook until most of sauce is absorbed. Serves 3 - 4

Scalloped Corn

An easy vegetable casserole

2 eggs, beaten
1 (14.75-ounce) can Del Monte cream-style corn
1 cup milk
¼ teaspoon salt

Freshly ground black pepper to taste
3 tablespoons butter
1 cup gluten-free bread crumbs (see beginning of Sides for recipe)

Preheat oven to 350°. Mix together eggs, corn, milk, salt and pepper. Pour in casserole dish. Melt butter and combine with bread crumbs. Sprinkle on top of casserole. Place casserole dish in pan of hot water. Bake 45 minutes or until set. Serves 4

SIDES

Simple Yellow Squash

1 tablespoon extra-virgin olive oil
1 large onion, chopped
2 garlic cloves, minced

8 medium yellow squash, halved length-wise and sliced
½-1 teaspoon Italian seasoning
Salt and pepper to taste

Heat oil in large skillet over medium heat. Add onion and garlic, and sauté 5-10 minutes. Add squash and cook 5 minutes. Add Italian seasoning, salt and pepper. Stir to mix well and continue cooking until squash reaches desired tenderness. Serves 3 - 4

Spinach with Raisins and Pine Nuts

2 pounds baby spinach (pre-washed bags work well)
¼ cup extra-virgin olive oil
¼ cup pine nuts

1 garlic clove, finely minced
¼ cup raisins
Salt and pepper to taste

Rinse and drain spinach, but do not completely dry.

Sprinkle wet spinach with salt and place in large saucepan. Cover and cook over medium heat until just wilted, about 5 minutes. Remove from heat.

Heat oil in skillet. Add pine nuts and cook until lightly browned. Add garlic, cook 1 minute and add spinach, raisins, salt and pepper. Heat about 3 minutes, stirring frequently. Serves 4

Notes:

SIDES

Steamed Butternut Squash and Fennel

These two vegetables complement each other well.

1 medium butternut squash, peeled and seeded
1 fennel bulb, stalks and bottom cut off
¼ cup parsley, chopped
1-2 tablespoons butter
Salt and pepper

Place steamer basket over pot of boiling water. Cut squash into 2-inch squares. Slice fennel bulb into 2-inch lengths. Place squash in steamer basket and steam about 5 minutes. Add fennel pieces, and continue steaming until vegetables are tender.

Pour vegetables into warm bowl. Add parsley, butter, salt and pepper to taste, and gently toss. Serves 6

Sweet and Sour Cabbage

Prepare a few hours ahead of time to allow flavors to blend.

1 (2-pound) head of cabbage
1 small onion
2 tablespoons extra-virgin olive oil
1½ teaspoons salt, divided
6 tablespoons white vinegar
1½ teaspoons caraway seeds
1-2 tablespoons sugar, or to taste

Slice cabbage and onion very thinly. Heat oil over medium-high heat in large stockpot. All remaining ingredients will be added in one-third increments. Put ⅓ of sliced cabbage and onion into pot, and sprinkle with ½ teaspoon salt, 2 tablespoons vinegar and ½ teaspoon caraway seeds. Stir often until cabbage collapses making room for more. Add another ⅓ of cabbage and onion, and repeat flavorings. Work raw cabbage and onion under collapsed cabbage. Sprinkle a little sugar over cabbage and stir well. Add remaining cabbage, onions and flavorings, and repeat process. Stir in a bit more sugar. Cook uncovered 35-40 minutes over medium heat, stirring occasionally. Taste and adjust. Serves 4

SIDES

Sweet Potato Risotto

1 small onion, finely chopped
3 garlic cloves, minced
3 tablespoons extra-virgin olive oil, divided
2 small sweet potatoes, peeled and grated
¾ cup Arborio rice

Freshly ground black pepper
3 cups vegetable broth*, heated
½ cup white wine
½ cup Parmesan cheese, freshly grated
Fresh parsley, finely chopped for garnish

Sauté onions and garlic in 1 tablespoon oil in large pot. Add remaining oil and potatoes, and sauté 2 minutes. Add rice and sauté 2 minutes more. Add pepper and heated vegetable broth one cup at a time; never add cold broth. Bring to boil, stirring constantly. Keep rice mixture boiling at all times. After adding all vegetable broth, add wine and continue stirring constantly. When risotto is smooth and creamy, stir in Parmesan cheese and mound onto serving plate. Garnish with fresh chopped parsley. Serves 4

*Pacific Natural Vegetable Broth is a gluten-free brand.

Notes:

SIDES

Sweet Potatoes with Orange Glaze

4 medium sweet potatoes, washed
2 tablespoons brown sugar

2 tablespoons butter
2 tablespoons orange juice concentrate*

Preheat oven to 375°. Line baking pan with aluminum foil and place potatoes in pan. Poke each potato twice with sharp knife. Bake 1 hour or until potatoes are soft.

Slice potatoes in half length-wise and cool. Scoop out insides, place in bowl and mash.

Heat brown sugar, butter and orange juice concentrate in small saucepan until mixture forms glaze, 3-5 minutes.

Butter 9-inch pie plate. Place potatoes in pie plate, level and smooth. Pour orange glaze over potatoes. Heat in oven 5-10 minutes. Serves 6

Minute Maid is gluten free.

White Rice with Mushrooms

Easily doubled for a dinner party

1 cup long-grain rice, uncooked
1 teaspoon oregano
2 (4-ounce) cans sliced mushrooms and
   liquid

½ cup butter
2½ cups beef broth*

Preheat oven to 400°. Sauté rice, oregano, mushrooms and liquid in butter 5-10 minutes. Put mixture in casserole dish and add beef broth. Bake 1 hour. Serve 5 - 6

Pacific Natural Foods Beef Broth is a gluten-free brand.

SIDES

White Rice with Peas

1 medium onion, chopped
1 tablespoon extra-virgin olive oil
2 cups cooked peas
¼-½ teaspoon crushed red pepper

3½ cups rice, cooked with 1 teaspoon extra-virgin olive oil
1 teaspoon garlic salt
Freshly ground black pepper to taste

Sauté onion in oil over medium heat 3-5 minutes. Add peas and red pepper, and sauté several minutes. Add rice, garlic salt and black pepper. Stir well and heat through. Serves 6

Zucchini and Sweet Onion Sauté

1 large sweet onion, chopped
2 garlic cloves, chopped
2 tablespoons extra-virgin olive oil
6 medium zucchini, halved length-wise and sliced

1-1½ teaspoons Italian seasoning
Salt to taste
Freshly ground black pepper to taste

Sauté onions and garlic in oil in large skillet over medium heat until tender. Add zucchini, sprinkle with Italian seasoning, salt and pepper, and stir well. Sauté 10-15 minutes, stirring often. Serves 4 - 6

Notes:

Notes

main dishes

Main Dishes

Beef

Beef and Turkey Chili with Corn
Beef Strips Oriental
Hungarian Goulash
Marinated Grilled Flank Steak
Meatloaf with Thyme
Mexican Beef with Rice
Sake-Marinated Filet Mignons
Simple Meatloaf with Bacon
Sloppy Joes
Stuffed Green Peppers
Swedish Meatballs in Cream Cheese Sauce
Texas Beef Chili

Lamb

Marinated Leg of Lamb

Poultry

Pan Gravy for Poultry
Apricot Chicken
Brined Roasted Turkey
Brunswick Stew
Chicken and Artichokes
Chicken Barbeque Sauce
Chicken Parmesan
Chicken Pot Pie
Chicken with Asian Marinade
Chinese Chicken
Curried Chicken Casserole
Grilled Chicken Tenders
Hot Chicken Salad Casserole
Hot Chicken Supreme
Mandarin Chicken with Black Beans
Southwestern Chicken
Specialty Chicken with Artichokes
Stir-Fry Chicken
Sweet and Sour Chicken
Turkey Tenderloins
White Chili
Zesty Chicken and Sausage Stew

Pork

Asian Pork Tenderloins
Baked Ham with Sweet Potatoes and Apples
Grilled Pork Tenderloin with Rosemary and Fennel Seeds
Ham Roll-Ups
Herb and Onion Pork Tenderloin

Pork Chops with Lime Sauce
Pork Chops with Tropical Sauce
Pork Loin Roast with Allspice and Thyme
Pork Medallions in Vermouth with Coriander
Raisin Sauce for Ham

Seafood
Fish Filets in Foil Packets
Lemony Orange Roughy
Sautéed Shrimp and Mushrooms
Shrimp and Scallops with Wild Rice
Shrimp Curry
Shrimp Provencal
Shrimp Salad
Shrimp with Roasted Red Pepper Cream
Steamed Salmon with Hollandaise Sauce

Pasta
Asian Pasta Stir-Fry
Baked Chicken Pasta with Pesto
Carbonara Pasta with Prosciutto and Peas
Fire Roasted Tomato and Beef Pasta
Italian Chicken Pasta for Two
Lasagna
Pasta Alfredo
Pasta Salad
Pasta with Artichoke Sauce
Pasta with Tuna Sauce
Sesame Flank Steak with Pasta
Zucchini Pasta

Vegetarian
Black Beans and Rice Cubano
Bok Choy Sesame Stir-Fry
Cauliflower and Broccoli Stir-Fry
Italian Vegetable Stew
Spicy Tofu Stir-Fry

MAIN DISHES

BEEF

Beef and Turkey Chili with Corn

A robust and flavorful chili prepared without beans

2 teaspoons extra-virgin olive oil	½ teaspoon oregano
½ sweet onion, diced	1 teaspoon salt
1½ pounds ground turkey	1 teaspoon freshly ground black pepper
1½ pounds ground beef	¼ cup honey
2 teaspoons chili powder	2 garlic cloves, minced
2 teaspoons rice flour	1 (6-ounce) can tomato paste
½ teaspoon cumin	1 (14.5-ounce) can diced tomatoes
¾ teaspoon crushed red pepper	1 (14.5-ounce) can tomato sauce
¾ teaspoon paprika	1½ cups frozen corn

Heat stockpot over medium heat. Add oil and onion, and sauté 5 minutes, stirring occasionally. Add meats and brown, stirring to cook evenly.

Combine chili powder, flour, cumin, red pepper, paprika, oregano, salt and pepper in small bowl and add to stockpot. Add honey and garlic and stir well.

Add tomato paste, diced tomatoes, tomato sauce and corn. Cover pot and simmer 30 minutes, stirring occasionally. Serves 6

Notes:

Main Dishes

Beef Strips Oriental

3 tablespoons extra-virgin olive oil, divided
1 pound sirloin steak, ¾-inch thick, cut into 2-inch strips, ¼-inch wide
3 garlic cloves, pressed
2 tablespoons ginger, freshly grated
1 large green pepper, cut into thin strips
3 stalks celery, cut on diagonal into 1-inch pieces
1 large onion, thinly sliced
5 small green onions, cut into 1½-inch lengths
2 cups broccoli, cut into florets
¼ teaspoon red pepper flakes
¼ cup soy sauce*
½ cup beef broth**
2 tablespoons dry sherry
12 cherry tomatoes
4 servings rice, cooked

Heat 2 tablespoons oil in large skillet, brown steak and remove. Place 1 tablespoon oil in skillet, add garlic and ginger, and sauté 1 minute. Add green pepper, celery, both onions, broccoli, red pepper flakes, soy sauce, broth, sherry and browned steak. Cook on low 20 minutes. Add cherry tomatoes and cook 2 minutes more. Serve over cooked rice. Serves 4

*La Choy and San-J are gluten free.
**Pacific Natural Foods Beef Broth is a gluten-free brand.

Notes:

MAIN DISHES

Hungarian Goulash

2½ pounds stew beef, in bite-sized pieces
Salt and pepper to taste
⅓ cup rice flour
2-3 tablespoons extra-virgin olive oil
2 large onions, chopped
6 garlic cloves, minced
⅓ cup paprika
1 jalapeño pepper, whole
2 plum tomatoes, quartered
2 cups beef broth*
3-4 carrots, in bite-sized pieces
2 parsnips, in bite-sized pieces
3-4 small potatoes, in bite-sized pieces
1 large green pepper, chopped
1 teaspoon caraway seeds
1 teaspoon salt, or to taste
8 ounces gluten-free pasta spirals, cooked (optional)

Salt and pepper beef, dredge in flour and shake off excess. Heat oil in large Dutch oven over medium-high heat. Add beef in batches and brown on all sides, being careful not to crowd pan or scorch meat. Remove meat with slotted spoon.

Add onions and cook over medium heat until lightly colored and soft, adding more oil if needed. Add garlic and sauté 1–2 minutes. Follow with paprika and stir well to coat onions and garlic thoroughly.

Return meat to skillet and stir, cooking over medium heat 10-15 minutes and then add jalapeño pepper, tomatoes and broth. Stir well, lower heat and simmer 1 hour. Add carrots, parsnips, potatoes, green pepper, caraway seeds and salt. Stir well. Continue to simmer 15-20 minutes. Remove jalapeño pepper. Serve over cooked pasta, if desired. Serves 6 - 8

Pacific Natural Foods Beef Broth is a gluten-free brand.

Notes:

MAIN DISHES

Marinated Grilled Flank Steak

2 garlic cloves, minced
½ teaspoon salt
1½ teaspoons dried rosemary
½ teaspoon ground ginger

½ cup Dijon mustard
2 tablespoons soy sauce*
1½-2 pounds flank steak or London Broil

Mash garlic, salt, rosemary and ginger in small bowl with back of spoon. Stir in mustard and soy sauce. Spread on both sides of meat. Refrigerate at least two hours. Preheat oven to broil or prepare grill. Broil or grill meat 5 minutes on each side, or longer if less rare is preferred. Cool and cut meat into slices against grain at angle. Serves 3 - 4

*La Choy and San-J are gluten free.

Meatloaf with Thyme

1 tablespoon vegetable oil
¼ cup onion, finely chopped
1 cup gluten-free bread crumbs (see beginning of Sides for recipe)
1-1¼ pounds ground beef or turkey
1 egg, beaten

¼ cup ketchup or applesauce
1 teaspoon Lea and Perrins Worcestershire sauce
½ teaspoon dried thyme
1 teaspoon salt
¼ teaspoon freshly ground black pepper

Preheat oven to 350°. Heat oil in small frying pan, add onions and sauté until lightly browned. Place all ingredients in food processor and process until well blended. Remove from food processor and place in lightly oiled baking pan. Form into rectangular loaf and bake 50-60 minutes. To test for doneness after 50 minutes, cut loaf in half. Meat should be browned all the way through. If still pink in middle, separate into halves and bake 5 minutes longer. Serves 4 - 6

Notes:

MAIN DISHES

Mexican Beef with Rice

1 tablespoon extra-virgin olive oil
1 large onion, chopped
1 pound lean ground beef
1 (16-ounce) jar salsa, medium or hot
1 (8-ounce) can tomato sauce
1 Herb-ox chicken bouillon cube or packet
4 servings white rice, cooked

Fresh tomatoes, chopped, or 1 (14.5 ounce) can diced tomatoes
Sour cream
Cheddar cheese, freshly grated
Black olives, sliced
Gluten-free tortilla chips

Heat oil in large skillet over medium heat. Add onions and sauté 10 minutes. Increase heat to medium-high, add ground beef and cook until browned. Add salsa, tomato sauce and bouillon. Reduce heat to low, cover and simmer 5 minutes. Serve over rice and pass tomatoes, sour cream, cheddar cheese and olives as garnishes. Serve with tortilla chips. Serves 4

Sake-Marinated Filet Mignons

4 (8-10 ounce) filet mignons
¼ cup soy sauce*

1¼ cups Sake (rice wine)
2 garlic cloves, minced

Place steaks in casserole dish. Mix soy sauce and sake and pour over steaks. Sprinkle with ½ minced garlic. Marinate 30-60 minutes. Turn, sprinkle again with remaining minced garlic and marinate 30-60 minutes. Sear each side of steaks on hot grill. Turn heat down and grill until preferred temperature. Serves 4

*La Choy and San-Jay are gluten free.

Notes:

Main Dishes

Simple Meatloaf with Bacon

1 pound lean ground beef
1 medium onion, chopped
1 teaspoon salt
Freshly ground black pepper to taste
1 (8-ounce) can tomato sauce

1 egg
2 slices gluten-free bread*, cubed
Gluten-free cooking spray
2 slices bacon

Preheat oven to 350°. Mix all ingredients in large bowl, except cooking spray and bacon. Shape into loaf and place in sprayed loaf pan. Top with bacon slices. Bake 45-50 minutes. Allow to cool 10 minutes before slicing. Serves 4 - 6

*Gluten-free bread is found in the freezer section.

Sloppy Joes

This recipe can be doubled or tripled for a crowd.

1 pound ground beef or turkey
1 small onion, finely chopped
1 cup celery, finely chopped
1 tablespoon red wine vinegar
1 cup ketchup

1 teaspoon salt
2 tablespoons sugar
2 tablespoons McCormick dry mustard
Gluten-free hamburger buns or bread*

Put all ingredients, except buns or bread, in pot and simmer 45-60 minutes uncovered. Stir occasionally. Serve on gluten-free hamburger buns or bread slices. Serves 4

*Gluten-free bread is found in the freezer section.

Notes:

Main Dishes

Stuffed Green Peppers

6 large green peppers
¼ cup extra-virgin olive oil
½ cup onion, chopped
1 large garlic clove, minced
1 pound lean ground beef
¾ cup Parmesan cheese, freshly grated

2 cups white rice, cooked
3 tablespoons parsley, chopped
Salt and pepper to taste
3 tablespoons red wine
1½ cups tomato juice

Preheat oven to 350°. Slice stem end from peppers and carefully remove seeds and pith. Parboil 5 minutes before stuffing. Heat oil in large skillet. Add onion and garlic, and sauté until onion is transparent. Add beef and cook until browned. Remove from heat. Stir in remaining ingredients except tomato juice, and let cool slightly. Stuff peppers with mixture. Place stuffed peppers in greased baking dish and pour tomato juice over and around peppers. Bake 30-40 minutes, basting occasionally with pan juices, adding more tomato juice if needed. Serves 6

Notes:

MAIN DISHES

Swedish Meatballs in Cream Cheese Sauce

A green salad with vinaigrette dressing complements this entrée.

1 pound ground beef
1 egg
½ cup gluten-free breadcrumbs (see beginning of Sides for recipe)
2 tablespoons onions, grated
½ teaspoon nutmeg
Salt and pepper to taste

2 tablespoons vegetable oil
1 (3-ounce) package cream cheese
½ cup water
⅛ teaspoon thyme
¾ cup milk
2 tablespoons parsley, chopped
Gluten-free pasta, cooked

Mix beef, egg, breadcrumbs, onion, nutmeg, salt and pepper in medium bowl. Shape beef mixture into 1-inch balls and brown in oil in skillet over medium heat until cooked through. Remove to bowl.

Pour off all but 2 tablespoons of drippings from skillet. Cut cream cheese into chunks and place in skillet with remaining ingredients except pasta. Cook over low heat, stirring with wire whisk until mixture is melted and smooth. Return meatballs to skillet; heat, stirring occasionally. Serve over pasta. Serves 4

Notes:

Main Dishes

Texas Beef Chili

Good for a crowd on a cold winter's night

2½ pounds lean ground beef
2 tablespoons extra-virgin olive oil
2 cups onions, chopped
1 green bell pepper, chopped
3 garlic cloves, minced
3 tablespoons chili powder
2 teaspoons dried oregano leaves
1½ teaspoons dried basil leaves
¼ teaspoon crushed red pepper
1-2 teaspoons ground cumin

2 teaspoons sugar
2 teaspoons salt
2 (14.5-ounce) cans diced tomatoes
2 (8-ounce) cans tomato sauce
1 (6-ounce) can tomato paste
2 (16-ounce) cans kidney beans, drained
8-10 servings rice, cooked
Cheddar cheese, freshly grated (optional)
Green onions, chopped (optional)

Brown beef in oil in Dutch oven over medium-high heat. Add onions, green pepper, garlic, chili powder, oregano, basil, red pepper and cumin. Mix well and cook 5 minutes or until onion and green peppers are tender, stirring often. Add sugar, salt, tomatoes, tomato sauce and paste, and mix well. Bring to boil, lower heat, cover and simmer slowly 40 minutes, stirring occasionally. Add beans, cover and simmer 10 more minutes or until hot. Serve over cooked rice. Top with grated cheddar cheese and/or chopped green onions, if desired. Serves 10 - 12

Notes:

MAIN DISHES

LAMB

Marinated Leg of Lamb

Marinating gives the lamb a mild taste.

6-7 pound leg of lamb, boned
3-4 garlic cloves, slivered

1 (16-ounce) bottle gluten-free Italian dressing

Cut slits in lamb and insert garlic slivers. Put lamb in large sealable plastic bag, add salad dressing. Marinate overnight in refrigerator. Bring lamb to room temperature before cooking. Preheat oven to 350°. Remove lamb from bag and bake 2 hours or until meat thermometer registers 180°. Lamb can also be cooked on grill. Serves 8-10

Notes:

Main Dishes

Poultry

Pan Gravy for Poultry

¼ cup poultry fat from pan
Pan juices
1-2 cups chicken broth*

2 tablespoons rice flour
Salt and pepper to taste

After roasting poultry, remove from pan. Pour off fat from roasting pan and reserve ¼ cup. Also, pour off remaining pan juices and reserve separately.

Place fat in sauté pan and stir in flour. Cook several minutes, stirring constantly. Slowly add reserved pan juices and enough chicken broth to make 2 cups, stirring constantly. Cook, stirring until gravy is thickened to desired consistency. Strain through fine-mesh sieve to remove lumps, if necessary. Add salt and pepper, and serve hot.

Pacific Natural Foods Chicken Broth is a gluten-free brand.

Notes:

MAIN DISHES

Apricot Chicken

Apricots and ginger add a distinctive flavor to the chicken.

1 cup dried apricots, diced
½ teaspoon ground ginger
1 cup dry white wine
6 tablespoons butter, divided
½ cup celery, chopped

1 medium onion, chopped
1 cup gluten-free bread crumbs (see beginning of Sides for recipe)
1 teaspoon poultry seasoning
1 organic roasting chicken

Soak apricots overnight in ginger and dry white wine. Drain apricots, reserving liquid. Sauté celery and onions in 2 tablespoons butter.

Preheat oven to 325°. Combine celery, onion, apricots and bread crumbs. Stuff chicken with mixture and place in roasting pan. Mix apricot/wine liquid, poultry seasoning and 4 tablespoons butter (melted). Baste chicken and bake 2½-3 hours, or until thigh pulls away from body. Baste occasionally. Serves 4

Notes:

MAIN DISHES

Brined Roasted Turkey

Brining keeps the turkey tender and moist

1 (12-14 pound) turkey, thawed, giblets and excess fat removed
1 cup kosher salt
2 gallons cold water
2 medium onions, coarsely chopped
2 medium carrots, coarsely chopped
2 celery stalks, coarsely chopped
4 garlic cloves, minced
4 tablespoons butter, melted
Gluten-free cooking spray
Pan Gravy (see beginning of Poultry for recipe)

The day before roasting:

Place turkey in large pot. Mix salt and water, and pour over turkey. Add more water and salt if needed to cover turkey. Cover and refrigerate at least 16-18 hours. (Turkey may be placed in a clean cooler. Use ice water or place ice packs in with brine. If more water is needed, add ½ cup kosher salt per gallon water.)

The day of roasting:

Preheat oven to 400°. Remove turkey from brine, rinse and pat dry. Place half of onions, carrots, celery and garlic inside turkey. Spray large roasting pan and spread remaining onions, carrots, celery and garlic in pan. Pour 1½ cups water over vegetables in pan. Place V-rack in pan and place turkey, breast side down, on rack. Brush back and sides with melted butter and roast 45 minutes. Remove pan from oven and baste turkey's back with caramelized vegetables in pan. Using several paper towels at each end of turkey, turn turkey on its side. Brush turkey again with pan drippings. Add ½ cup water to pan and return to oven.

Remove turkey from oven after 20 minutes and turn again so the other leg and wing face up. Baste with drippings, add ½ cup water to pan and return to oven. After another 20 minutes remove turkey from oven. Turn to put breast side up and baste with drippings. Add ½ cup water to pan and return to oven. Lower heat to 325° and roast 60-75 minutes longer, until a meat thermometer inserted in breast registers 160°-165°. Allow turkey to cool 30 minutes before carving. Serve with gravy. Serves 6 - 8

MAIN DISHES

Brunswick Stew

Flavor is enhanced when made a day ahead.

1 (32-ounce) carton chicken broth*
2 cups water
2 Herb-ox chicken bouillon cubes
2½ cups frozen corn kernels
1½ cups frozen baby lima beans
2½ cups potatoes, cubed
2 cups onion, chopped
4 slices bacon, chopped

1 (14-ounce) can diced tomatoes
3-4 cups cooked organic chicken, in bite-sized pieces
1 teaspoon sweet paprika
1 teaspoon sugar
½ -1 teaspoon salt, or to taste
½ teaspoon freshly ground black pepper
¼ teaspoon red pepper flakes

Combine broth, water, bouillon, corn and lima beans in large pot. Begin heating over medium-low heat while adding potatoes, onions, bacon and diced tomatoes to pot. Bring to boil, lower heat and simmer 15 minutes. Add cooked chicken, paprika, sugar, salt, black pepper and red pepper flakes. Bring to boil again, reduce heat and simmer another 10-15 minutes. Serves 6 - 8

*Pacific Natural Foods Chicken Broth is a gluten-free brand.

Notes:

MAIN DISHES

Chicken and Artichokes

This recipe makes a beautiful presentation.

4 large boneless, skinless, organic chicken breasts
2 tablespoons vegetable oil
1 medium red pepper, cut into thin strips
1 (9-ounce) package frozen artichoke hearts
¼ cup mayonnaise*
2 teaspoons red wine vinegar
2 teaspoons Dijon mustard
½ teaspoon Herb-ox chicken bouillon
⅔ cups water

Pound breasts to ½-inch. Heat oil in 12-inch skillet over medium heat and add red pepper. Cook until tender and remove. Add chicken to skillet and lightly brown, about 8 minutes, and remove. Keep peppers and chicken warm in low oven.

Prepare artichokes according to package directions and drain. Combine mayonnaise, vinegar, mustard, bouillon and water in small bowl. Using wire whisk, blend until smooth. Pour mixture into skillet. Cook until smooth and mixture comes to boil. Pour sauce on platter; arrange chicken and artichokes over sauce. Garnish with red pepper strips. Serves 4

Kraft and Hellmann's are gluten free.

Chicken Barbeque Sauce

This recipe may be increased – just use twice as much vinegar as oil.

1 cup vegetable oil
2 cups vinegar, either red or white
1 tablespoon salt
1 tablespoon freshly ground black pepper
1 tablespoon poultry seasoning

Mix all ingredients together and heat. Baste chicken regularly. Works well if chicken is baked in oven 1 hour and put on grill to finish. Makes 3 cups

MAIN DISHES

Chicken Parmesan

Great either for dinner with a salad or in smaller strips as an appetizer

⅔ cup Parmesan cheese, freshly grated
⅓ cup rice flour
1 teaspoon sweet basil
1 teaspoon paprika
½ teaspoon garlic powder
½ teaspoon salt (optional)

1 teaspoon freshly ground black pepper
1 egg
1 tablespoon milk
4-6 boneless, skinless, organic chicken breasts, cut into thirds
¼ cup butter, melted

Preheat oven to 350°. Mix together cheese, flour, basil, paprika, garlic, salt and pepper in shallow bowl. Blend egg and milk in another shallow bowl. Wash chicken and pat dry. Dip chicken in egg mixture, then coat with cheese/flour mixture. Place in baking dish, pour melted butter over chicken. Bake 45-60 minutes. Serves 4

Notes:

Main Dishes

Chicken Pot Pie

Eliminating the traditional crust makes this an easy recipe to prepare.

Crust topping:

2 cups almond flour
5 tablespoons butter, melted

1 egg yolk

Combine almond flour, butter and egg yolk in small bowl and set aside.

Pie Filling:

¼ cup peas
¼ cup carrots, finely chopped
¼ cup celery, finely chopped
1 cup chicken broth*
1 whole egg, plus 2 egg yolks

⅓ cup yogurt
2 ½ cups boneless, skinless, organic chicken breast, cooked and chopped
½ cup Gouda cheese, freshly grated

Preheat oven to 350°. Place peas, carrots, celery and broth in saucepan, bring to boil and simmer 10 minutes. Using slotted spoon, remove cooked vegetables, saving broth.

Place egg and yolks in small bowl. While beating continuously, pour small stream of hot broth into bowl. (This will prevent eggs from clumping and will insure smooth custard consistency.) When enough broth has been added to warm eggs well, pour contents of bowl back into saucepan. Cook until sauce thickens. Add yogurt and stir well.

Butter 9-inch pie pan. Add cooked chicken, vegetables and cheese, distributing evenly. Pour sauce over chicken mixture and sprinkle crust topping evenly over pot pie. Bake 45 minutes or until crust topping is lightly browned. Serves 4

*Pacific Natural Foods Chicken Broth is a gluten-free brand.

MAIN DISHES

Chicken with Asian Marinade

This has both a hint of sweetness from honey and a little tang from ginger. To save time, prepare marinade the night before, but do not combine with meat until morning. It works equally well with flank steak.

3-4 boneless, skinless, organic chicken breasts	2 teaspoons toasted sesame oil
3 tablespoons fresh ginger, peeled and shredded	1 teaspoon extra-virgin olive oil
	1 teaspoon red wine vinegar
	¼ cup honey
2 green onions, chopped	1 teaspoon salt
1 garlic clove, minced	¼ cup water

Cut chicken breasts in half and trim off any visible fat. Place chicken in bowl or gallon-sized, ziploc bag and refrigerate.

Place ginger, green onions and garlic in medium bowl. Add sesame oil, olive oil, vinegar, honey, salt and water, and blend well. Pour marinade over chicken and stir to coat all surfaces. Marinate 6-8 hours, but not overnight. Remove chicken pieces and place directly on grill. Cook until chicken is lightly browned, firm when pressed and no longer pink on inside. Serves 3 - 4

Notes:

MAIN DISHES

Chinese Chicken

A nice blend of tastes and textures

3 boneless, skinless, organic chicken breasts, cubed
2 tablespoons extra-virgin olive oil or sesame oil
¾ cup green pepper, chopped
¾ cup green onion, chopped
1 (5-ounce) can sliced water chestnuts, drained
¾ cup celery, chopped
1 cup sliced mushrooms
2 tablespoons soy sauce* or to taste
4 servings brown rice, cooked

Sauté chicken in oil until tender. Add all vegetables and soy sauce to mixture and stir until vegetables are just crisp. Serve over brown rice. Serves 4

*La Choy and San-J are gluten free.

Curried Chicken Casserole

3 large boneless, skinless, organic chicken breasts
2 tablespoons extra-virgin olive oil
1 cup celery, chopped
2½ cups rice, cooked
1 medium onion, finely diced
1 cup mayonnaise*
2 tablespoons McCormick curry powder
1 cup sherry
Salt and pepper to taste
1 (4-ounce) can mushrooms

Preheat oven to 350°. Sauté chicken in oil and cut into cubes. Mix all ingredients together in casserole dish and bake 45 minutes. Serves 8

*Kraft and Hellmann's are gluten free.

Notes:

MAIN DISHES

Grilled Chicken Tenders

Serve as a main entrée or as an addition to a green salad.

3-4 boneless, skinless, organic chicken tenders per serving

Balsamic vinaigrette (see beginning of Salads for recipe)

Place chicken tenders in casserole dish. Pour vinaigrette over chicken and toss to make sure tenders are coated. Cover dish and refrigerate 2-4 hours. Spray indoor grill and heat for recommended time. Place chicken tenders on grill, close lid and grill 5-6 minutes.

Hot Chicken Salad Casserole

This may also be made with turkey or tuna.

5-6 slices gluten-free bread*
2 cups boneless, skinless, organic chicken, cooked and cubed
2 cups celery, thinly sliced
½ cup slivered almonds
¼ cup onions, minced
½ teaspoon salt
2 tablespoons fresh lemon juice

1 cup mayonnaise**
½ cup cheddar or Swiss cheese, freshly grated
¼ teaspoon parsley
¼ teaspoon sage
¼ teaspoon rosemary
¼ teaspoon thyme

Preheat oven to 375°. Butter bread slices, remove crusts and cut slices into cubes. Bake until crisp, about 10-15 minutes.

Increase oven temperature to 450°. Mix all ingredients except 1 cup croutons and cheese. Spoon mixture into casserole dish and sprinkle with remaining croutons and cheese. Bake 10-15 minutes or until bubbly. Serves 6

Gluten-free bread is found in the freezer section.
**Kraft and Hellmann's are gluten free.*

MAIN DISHES

Hot Chicken Supreme

Delicious for an informal dinner accompanied with good conversation and salad

3 boneless, skinless, organic chicken breasts, cooked and diced
1 cup celery, chopped
¾ cup sharp cheddar cheese, freshly grated
¾ cup mayonnaise*
¼ cup milk
¼ cup slivered almonds, toasted

¼ cup pimiento, chopped
2 tablespoons dry sherry
1½ teaspoons onion, chopped
¼ teaspoon poultry seasoning
¼ teaspoon lemon rind, grated
⅓ cup gluten-free bread crumbs (see beginning of Sides for recipe)

Preheat oven to 350°. Combine all ingredients except bread crumbs. Stir well. Put mixture in greased 2-quart casserole and top with bread crumbs. Bake 30 minutes. Serves 4

*Kraft and Hellmann's are gluten free.

Notes:

Main Dishes

Mandarin Chicken with Black Beans

1 tablespoon extra-virgin olive oil
4 skinned, boned organic chicken breast halves, cut in bite-sized pieces
½ teaspoon salt
1 medium onion, chopped
3 garlic cloves, minced
⅓ cup orange juice*
Juice of one lime
2 (15-ounce) cans black beans, rinsed and drained
1 cup chicken broth**
4-6 servings brown rice, cooked in chicken broth** according to package directions
1 (15-ounce) can mandarin oranges, drained
Chopped fresh cilantro
4-6 servings rice, cooked

Heat oil in large nonstick skillet over medium-high heat. Add chicken pieces and salt, and cook until browned, about 5 minutes. Remove chicken with slotted spoon and set aside. Add onion and garlic to skillet and sauté 3-4 minutes. Add orange and lime juice, and cook 2 minutes. Stir in beans and broth. Add chicken, bring to boil, reduce heat and simmer 10 minutes. Serve over rice. Top with mandarin oranges and sprinkle with cilantro. Serves 4 - 6

*Tropicana is gluten free.
**Pacific Natural Foods Chicken Broth is a gluten-free brand.

Notes:

MAIN DISHES

Southwestern Chicken

4 boneless, skinless, organic chicken breasts halves
1 medium onion, chopped
2 teaspoons Lea & Perrins Worcestershire Sauce
2 teaspoons fresh lime juice
2 garlic cloves, minced

1 (14.5-ounce) can diced tomatoes
1 (4.5-ounce) can chopped green chilies
1 (15-ounce) can black beans, drained
1 cup rice
½ cup water
1 cup cheddar cheese, freshly grated
Fresh cilantro for garnish, chopped

Preheat oven to 350°. Place chicken and onions in greased 2-quart casserole. Mix Worcestershire Sauce, lime juice and garlic, and sprinkle over chicken and onions. Bake 30 minutes or until chicken is cooked through. Add tomatoes, green chilies, black beans, rice and water to casserole dish, and mix well. Cover dish tightly, return to oven and bake 45-60 minutes, or until rice is tender. Sprinkle with cheddar cheese. Garnish with cilantro. Serves 4

Notes:

Main Dishes

Specialty Chicken with Artichokes

An easy dish for company

4 boneless, skinless, organic chicken breasts
1 yellow onion, thinly sliced
2 tablespoons extra-virgin olive oil
1 (14-ounce) jar marinated artichoke hearts
1 (14.5-ounce) can diced tomatoes
6 tablespoons red wine vinegar
1 tablespoon garlic, minced
½ teaspoon salt
½ teaspoon freshly ground black pepper
4 servings rice or gluten-free pasta, cooked
Parmesan cheese, freshly grated

Sauté chicken and onions in oil in large skillet 5-10 minutes or until chicken is no longer pink in center. Add artichoke hearts with liquid, tomatoes, vinegar, garlic, salt and pepper. Simmer 30 minutes. Serve over rice or pasta. Sprinkle with cheese. Serves 4

Notes:

Main Dishes

Stir-Fry Chicken

2 tablespoons extra-virgin olive oil
1 cup celery, thinly sliced
1 green bell pepper, cut in thin strips
1 medium onion, halved and sliced
8 ounces fresh mushrooms, sliced
1 teaspoon salt
½ teaspoon ground ginger
4 boneless, skinless, organic chicken breast halves, sliced into ¼-inch strips

1 (14.5-ounce) can bean sprouts, drained
1 (5-ounce) can sliced water chestnuts, drained
1 Herb-ox chicken bouillon cube or packet
½ cup hot water
2 teaspoons cornstarch
2 tablespoons soy sauce*
4 servings rice, cooked
¾ cup slivered almonds, toasted

Heat oil in 12-inch skillet over medium-high heat. Add celery, pepper, onion, mushrooms, salt and ginger. Cook, stirring frequently, until vegetables are tender-crisp, about 3 minutes. With slotted spoon, remove vegetables and keep warm. Add chicken to skillet and stir-fry 3-5 minutes. Return vegetables to skillet. Add bean sprouts and water chestnuts. Dissolve chicken bouillon in water and add to mixture. Blend cornstarch with soy sauce until smooth, and gradually stir into hot mixture. Cook, stirring constantly, until thickened. Serve over hot rice. Top with almonds. Serves 4

*La Choy and San-J are gluten free.

Notes:

MAIN DISHES

Sweet and Sour Chicken

1 medium onion, thinly sliced
1 large green pepper, cut in strips
3 tablespoons butter
2 cups pineapple juice, divided
¼ cup brown sugar
¼ cup vinegar
3 tablespoons soy sauce*

⅛ teaspoon Tabasco
3 tablespoons cornstarch
2 cups skinless, boneless, organic chicken, cooked and diced
¼ cup carrots, cooked and sliced
1 (8-ounce) can pineapple chunks

Sauté onions and green pepper in butter 5 minutes. Add 1¾ cups pineapple juice and bring to boil. Stir in sugar, vinegar, soy sauce and Tabasco. In small bowl, combine remaining ¼ cup pineapple juice and cornstarch, and stir well. Gradually add to vegetable mixture. Bring mixture to boil, reduce heat and simmer three minutes. Add chicken, carrots and pineapple. Cook until thoroughly heated. Serves 3

*La Choy and San-J are gluten free.

Turkey Tenderloins

1 pound turkey tenderloins
¼ cup soy sauce*
¼ cup peanut oil
¼ cup cooking sherry
2 tablespoons lemon juice

2 teaspoons white pepper
2 tablespoons onion, chopped
2 teaspoons McCormick garlic powder or 2 garlic cloves, minced
2 teaspoons ground ginger

Place turkey in sealable plastic bag. Mix all remaining ingredients and add to bag. Place in refrigerator at least 24 hours, turning occasionally.

Cook tenderloins on low heat on grill 8-10 minutes per side. Cook until no pink color remains. Serves 2 - 3

*La Choy and San-J are gluten free.

Main Dishes

White Chili

An interesting alternative to regular chili

1 tablespoon extra-virgin olive oil
1 large onion, chopped
4-6 garlic cloves, minced
4 boneless, skinless, organic chicken breasts cut into bite-sized pieces
1 (4.5-ounce) can chopped green chilies
1 teaspoon ground cumin
1 teaspoon dried oregano
¼ teaspoon ground cloves
2 (16-ounce) cans Great Northern beans, drained
3 cups chicken broth*
Salt to taste
4 servings rice, cooked
Gluten-free chunky salsa

Heat oil in Dutch oven over medium-high heat. Sauté onions 5 minutes. Add garlic and chicken pieces. Sauté 5 minutes. Add chilies, cumin, oregano, cloves, beans, broth and salt. Bring to boil, reduce heat, cover and simmer 1 hour. Serve over rice and pass salsa. Serves 4

*Pacific Natural Foods Chicken Broth is a gluten-free brand.

Notes:

Main Dishes

Zesty Chicken and Sausage Stew

1 (16-ounce) package gluten-free smoked sausage, cut into bite-sized pieces
4 skinless, boneless, organic chicken breasts, cut into bite-sized pieces
2-3 tablespoons extra-virgin olive oil
1 large onion, chopped
1 large green bell pepper, chopped
3 garlic cloves, minced
1 (14.5-ounce) can diced tomatoes, undrained
2 bay leaves
1½ teaspoons thyme
¼ teaspoon salt
¼ teaspoon freshly ground black pepper
2 (16-ounce) cans Great Northern beans, undrained
1 Herb-ox chicken bouillon cube or packet
½ cup water

Brown sausage and chicken in oil in 6-quart Dutch oven 10 minutes. Remove with slotted spoon. Sauté onion, bell pepper and garlic until tender, 8-10 minutes. Add sausage, chicken, tomatoes, bay leaves, thyme, salt and pepper. Cover, reduce heat and simmer 10 minutes. Stir in beans, bouillon and water. Cover and continue cooking 10 minutes. Discard bay leaves before serving. Serves 6 - 8

Notes:

MAIN DISHES

PORK

Asian Pork Tenderloins

1 teaspoon gluten-free red or white miso*
1 tablespoon almond butter
⅓ cup boiling water
½ cup sesame seeds
2½ tablespoons sugar
1 tablespoon onion, minced
1 tablespoon ground ginger
½ teaspoon garlic powder
2 pork tenderloins**

Mix miso and almond butter in bowl, slowly adding hot water, and stirring until combined. Add sesame seeds, sugar, onion, ginger and garlic powder. Put tenderloins in sealable plastic bag, add sauce and marinate overnight. Heat oven to 375º. Remove meat from bag and bake 1 hour. Cool and slice thinly. Serve with miso-almond sauce.

Miso-Almond Sauce:

4 tablespoons gluten-free red or white miso*
6 tablespoons almond butter
1½ cups boiling water, divided

Place miso and almond butter in medium bowl. Add ½ cup hot water and mash with spoon until mixture becomes a paste. Add remaining water and mix until well combined. Serves 4

*Miso can be found in the refrigerator section of a health food store. Check label; some miso is made with barley.

** Use pork tenderloin without a basting solution injected into the meat. Read label carefully for gluten.

MAIN DISHES

Baked Ham with Sweet Potatoes and Apples

The sweet and salty flavors blend nicely in this easy-to-prepare casserole.

1½ pounds precooked ham, sliced
3 large sweet potatoes, peeled and sliced
5 baking apples*, peeled, cored and sliced

2 tablespoons brown sugar
2 tablespoons butter

Preheat oven to 350°. Butter 9 x 13-inch baking pan. Cover bottom with ham slices, then sweet potatoes and finally apples. Sprinkle brown sugar on top and dot with butter. Cover dish with foil. Bake 1 hour 45 minutes or until sweet potatoes are soft. Serves 6

*One 13.5-ounce can crushed pineapple with juice can be substituted for apples.

Grilled Pork Tenderloin with Rosemary and Fennel Seeds

2 (1-pound) pork tenderloins*
2 tablespoons extra-virgin olive oil
1 tablespoon fennel seeds, ground or crushed

2 teaspoons dried rosemary
2 teaspoons salt
1 teaspoon freshly ground black pepper

Place tenderloins on large plate and rub with oil. Blend together fennel seeds, rosemary, salt and pepper in small bowl. Rub seasoning mix over meat, pressing until seasoning adheres.

Grill tenderloins at 425° or medium-high heat until internal temperature reaches 150°. Remove from heat and let meat rest at least 5 minutes before slicing. Serves 4

*Use pork tenderloin without a basting solution injected into the meat. Read label carefully.

MAIN DISHES

Ham Roll-Ups

An easy casserole with a unique flavor

6 slices Boar's Head ham, ¼ inch thick
6 slices mozzarella cheese
1 (10-ounce) package frozen broccoli spears, cooked
6 tablespoons butter, divided
1 large onion, cut into rings

2 tablespoons rice flour
Dash salt
¼ teaspoon basil
Dash pepper
1 cup milk

Preheat oven to 350º. Top each ham slice with one slice cheese, place one broccoli spear on each and roll up. Secure with toothpick and place in greased shallow baking dish.

Melt 2 tablespoons butter in small saucepan and sauté onions until tender. Remove onions and spoon over roll-ups. Melt remaining butter. Blend flour and seasonings with butter, stirring constantly over low heat until well blended. Gradually add milk, continuing to stir. When mixture thickens, pour over roll-ups. Bake 25 minutes. Serves 3

Notes:

MAIN DISHES

Herb and Onion Pork Tenderloin

Delicious with Sweet and Sour Cabbage, page 113

Gluten-free cooking spray
2 (8-ounce) pork tenderloins*
2 medium onions, sliced and separated into rings
2 large garlic cloves, minced

2 teaspoons extra-virgin olive oil
½ teaspoon rosemary
¼ teaspoon thyme
¼ teaspoon salt
⅛ teaspoon freshly ground black pepper

Preheat oven to 375º. Spray roasting pan and rack with cooking spray. Trim fat from tenderloins and cut lengthwise slit down center of each, almost through to bottom. Open tenderloins so each lies flat and place on prepared rack. Sauté onions and garlic in hot oil until tender. Stir in rosemary, thyme, salt and pepper. Spread onion mixture evenly over tenderloins. Bake 40 minutes or until meat is no longer pink. Serves 4

Use pork tenderloin without a basting solution injected into the meat. Read label carefully.

Pork Chops with Lime Sauce

¼ cup fresh lime juice
2 tablespoons extra-virgin olive oil
1½ teaspoons fresh garlic, minced
¼ teaspoon oregano

Freshly ground black pepper to taste
1½ pounds boneless pork loin chops, about ¾-inch thick

Whisk together lime juice, oil, garlic, oregano and pepper. Place chops in single layer in glass dish. Pour mixture over pork chops and marinate covered 1 hour. Cook meat as desired: grilled, fried or broiled. Serves 4

Notes:

MAIN DISHES

Pork Chops with Tropical Sauce

The fruits and spices add an island flavor.

2 teaspoons McCormick curry powder
1 teaspoon ginger
¼ teaspoon cinnamon
1 cup dried fruit bits (mango, papaya, pineapple)
½ cup orange juice*
1 tablespoon vinegar

2 tablespoons pineapple or apricot gluten-free preserves
4 boneless top loin chops
Salt to taste
2 teaspoons extra-virgin olive oil
2 teaspoons butter

Stir together curry, ginger and cinnamon in bowl. Remove 1 teaspoon of spice mixture for sauce and reserve remaining mixture to season pork chops.

Mix together dried fruit, orange juice, vinegar and 1 teaspoon spice mixture in small sauce pan. Bring to boil, stirring often. Add preserves and stir to dissolve. Remove from heat, cover and let stand.

Pat pork chops dry with paper towels and sprinkle both sides lightly with salt. Rub spice mixture over both sides of chops. Warm oil and butter in 12-inch skillet over medium-high heat until butter turns golden brown. Add pork chops, cooking 3-4 minutes without moving or turning. Put sauce back on low heat before pork chops are done. Turn chops and brown 3-4 additional minutes. Serve immediately with reheated sauce. Serves 4

* Tropicana is gluten free.

Notes:

Main Dishes

Pork Loin Roast with Allspice and Thyme

1 tablespoon extra-virgin olive oil
2 teaspoons dried thyme
2 teaspoons ground allspice
1½ teaspoons salt
½ teaspoon freshly ground black pepper
1 (4-5 pound) pork loin roast, bone-in or boneless

Preheat oven to 450°. Mix together oil, thyme, allspice, salt and pepper in small bowl. Rub roast all over with seasoning mixture.

Place roast on rack in baking pan and place in oven. Roast 15 minutes at 450°; reduce oven temperature to 250°. Continue baking until thickest part of meat registers 155-160° on meat thermometer, additional 80-90 minutes. Remove pork roast from oven and let stand 10 minutes before carving. Serves 6 - 8

Notes:

Main Dishes

Pork Medallions in Vermouth with Coriander

1¼ pound pork filet, cut into 1-inch medallions
2 teaspoons ground coriander
1 tablespoon extra-virgin olive oil
2 tablespoons butter
1 sweet onion, finely chopped
1 Granny Smith or other tart apple, peeled, cored and finely chopped
Salt and freshly ground black pepper to taste
1 teaspoon sugar
5 ounces dry vermouth
5 ounces chicken broth*
2 egg yolks
1 tablespoon parsley, finely chopped

Preheat oven to 350º. Sprinkle pork medallions with coriander. Heat oil and butter in frying pan. Add pork and fry over high heat, 2-3 minutes to sear and brown. With slotted spoon, transfer pork to casserole dish. Add onion to pan and fry over low heat 5 minutes, until soft and lightly colored. Add apple and fry additional 2-3 minutes. Add salt, pepper, sugar, vermouth and broth to pork and stir well. Bake 45 minutes. Remove pork from casserole with slotted spoon, leaving onion and apple in liquid for sauce. Arrange medallions on serving dish and keep warm. Purée apples and onion with cooking liquid in blender and stir in egg yolks. Taste and adjust seasoning. Warm sauce over low heat in saucepan, but do not boil. Pour sauce over pork and sprinkle with parsley. Serves 4

*Pacific Natural Foods Chicken Broth is a gluten-free brand.

Notes:

MAIN DISHES

Raisin Sauce for Ham

An elegant addition to ham

1 cup raisins
¼ cup butter
2 cups water
4 tablespoons cider vinegar
2 teaspoons prepared mustard
2 tablespoons rice flour

½ cup brown sugar, packed
¼ teaspoon salt
¼ teaspoon ground cloves
1 teaspoon ground cinnamon

Rinse and drain raisins. Combine butter, water, vinegar and mustard, and heat to boiling. Blend together flour, sugar, salt, cloves and cinnamon, and stir into hot mixture. Add raisins and simmer 10 minutes. Serve hot over ham slices. Yields 2 cups

Notes:

MAIN DISHES

SEAFOOD

Fish Filets in Foil Packets

A versatile recipe for many kinds of mild fish - halibut, grouper, red snapper, salmon, tilapia or orange roughy

1 large leek, washed and trimmed	¼ cup water
1 large carrot, peeled	Salt and black pepper to taste
1-2 tablespoons butter	2 (5-7-ounce) fish filets

Preheat oven to 400°. Cut leek and carrot in half crosswise and slice into matchstick-sized pieces.

Melt butter in skillet. Add carrots and water, cover skillet and cook 5 minutes, stirring occasionally. Add leeks, salt and pepper, cover and cook about 5 minutes longer, until leeks are soft.

Cut two sheets of heavy-duty aluminum foil. Cover with slightly smaller pieces of parchment paper. In center of each, place one filet and half the vegetables. Fold and crimp edges.

Place foil packets on baking sheet and bake 10-18 minutes, depending on thickness of filets. To test for doneness, remove packet from oven and carefully open. Fish should flake easily with fork. Serves 2

Notes:

MAIN DISHES

Lemony Orange Roughy

A tangy but lightly flavored fish

Gluten-free cooking spray
4 orange roughy filets
2 tablespoons lemon juice
2 tablespoons brown or horseradish mustard
1½ tablespoons butter, melted
Freshly ground black pepper to taste
Lemon slices (optional)

Coat rack of broiler pan with gluten-free cooking spray. Place filets on rack. Combine lemon juice, mustard and butter. Spread mixture over filets. Broil filets 5-6 inches from heat 8-10 minutes or until fish flakes easily. Remove from broiler. Sprinkle lightly with pepper. Garnish with lemon slices. Serves 4

Sautéed Shrimp and Mushrooms

2 tablespoons butter
1 garlic clove, crushed
1 pound raw shrimp, peeled and deveined
½ cup fresh mushrooms, sliced
¼ cup dry sherry
4 servings rice, cooked

Melt butter and sauté garlic in skillet. Stir in shrimp, mushrooms and sherry. Bring to boil. Cover and simmer over low heat until shrimp are firm and pink about 3-4 minutes. DO NOT OVERCOOK. Serve over rice. Serves 4

Notes:

MAIN DISHES

Shrimp and Scallops with Wild Rice

2 tablespoons butter
1 pound medium shrimp, peeled and deveined
1 pound scallops
½ cup white wine
1 (4-ounce) can mushrooms, drained
½ cup celery, finely diced
½ cup cream
1 cup sour cream
8 ounces Swiss cheese, grated
Salt and pepper to taste
8 servings wild rice, cooked

Melt butter in skillet and sauté shrimp and scallops until shrimp begins to turn pink and curl. Add wine, reduce heat to medium and cook two minutes. Remove shrimp and scallops and set aside. Reduce heat to low. Combine mushrooms, celery, cream, sour cream, cheese, salt and pepper, and add to skillet. Stir until well-blended. Add shrimp and scallops and heat thoroughly. Serve over hot rice. Serves 8-10

Notes:

MAIN DISHES

Shrimp Curry

¼ cup butter
½ sweet onion, chopped
1 garlic clove, minced
4 teaspoons McCormick curry powder
½ teaspoon ground ginger
⅛ teaspoon ground cardamom
⅛ teaspoon cinnamon
⅛ teaspoon turmeric
⅛ teaspoon chili powder, or to taste
1 tablespoon rice flour
½ cup canned coconut milk

¾ cup chicken broth*
1 teaspoon lime zest, grated
1½ pounds large shrimp, peeled and deveined
1 tablespoon lime juice
Salt and pepper to taste
4 servings rice, cooked
Garnishes: raisins, salted roasted peanuts, chopped candied ginger
Mango chutney

Melt butter in heavy 5-quart pot over medium heat. Add onion and garlic, and cook, stirring until onion is softened, about 4 minutes.

Combine curry powder, ginger, cardamom, cinnamon, turmeric, chili powder and rice flour in small bowl. Add to pot and cook stirring constantly, about 2 minutes.

Stir coconut milk well and then measure. Whisk in coconut milk, chicken broth and lime zest. Bring just to boil and then simmer mixture, stirring constantly until it begins to thicken, about 2 minutes.

Add shrimp and simmer, stirring until shrimp turns pink and is cooked through, about 4 minutes. Stir in lime juice. Add salt and pepper.

Ladle curried shrimp over rice and top with garnishes. Serve chutney on the side. Serves 4

*Pacific Natural Foods Chicken Broth is a gluten-free brand.

MAIN DISHES

Shrimp Provençal

Serve as is, or spoon over cooked gluten-free pasta sprinkled with Parmesan cheese.

2 tablespoons extra-virgin olive oil
¼ teaspoon freshly ground black pepper
1 pound raw shrimp (20-24 count), peeled and deveined
½ teaspoon garlic, finely chopped
1½ teaspoons shallots, finely chopped

⅔ cup dry white wine
2 tablespoons lemon juice
⅓ teaspoon salt
4 tablespoons unsalted butter, softened
½ cup heavy cream
1 tablespoon parsley, finely chopped

Heat oil and add pepper. Sauté shrimp over low heat turning once until pink on both sides, about 3 minutes, stirring occasionally until shrimp browns slightly. Remove shrimp. Add garlic, shallots, wine, lemon juice and salt. Bring to boil and reduce liquid to not quite half. Return shrimp and heat through. Remove from heat; blend in butter and cream stirring until melted. Top with chopped parsley. Serves 2

Shrimp Salad

This can be served on gluten-free toast or as salad over lettuce with assorted garnishes.

1 pound raw shrimp, peeled, deveined and cooked
2 eggs, hard-boiled and chopped

1 cup celery, chopped
¼ cup mayonnaise*
Salt and pepper to taste

Chill shrimp at least 1 hour, cut each in half or thirds and place in bowl. Add eggs, celery and mayonnaise, and toss. Add salt and pepper. Chill until ready to serve. Serves 4

Kraft and Hellmann's are gluten free.

MAIN DISHES

Shrimp with Roasted Red Pepper Cream

Surprisingly good and very attractive to serve

8 ounces gluten-free pasta
1 (12-ounce) jar roasted red peppers, drained
8 ounces cream cheese, softened
¾ cup chicken broth*
3 garlic cloves, pressed

¼ - ½ teaspoon ground red pepper
2 pounds large shrimp, peeled, deveined, and cooked
¼ cup fresh basil, chopped
Fresh basil sprig for garnish

Prepare pasta according to package directions. While pasta is cooking, begin preparing sauce. Process red peppers, cream cheese, broth and garlic in blender or food processor until smooth. Pour mixture into large skillet. Cook over medium heat 5 minutes, stirring often until heated through. Add pepper and shrimp. Cook an additional 2-3 minutes, stirring occasionally. Remove from heat. Serve over hot cooked pasta. Sprinkle basil on top and garnish with basil sprig. Serves 4

*Pacific Natural Foods Chicken Broth is a gluten-free brand.

Notes:

MAIN DISHES

Steamed Salmon with Hollandaise Sauce

This recipe is quick, simple and quite elegant.

6 (4-ounce) salmon filets
1 cup white wine, room temperature

2 bay leaves

Preheat oven to 450º. Place salmon filets in 9 x 13-inch baking dish. Add wine and bay leaves. Cover with foil, and bake 8 minutes or until fish flakes with fork. If filets are thick, cooking time should be increased. Serve with Hollandaise sauce. Serves 6

Hollandaise Sauce:

½ cup butter
¼ cup hot water
¼ teaspoon salt

⅛ teaspoon white pepper
4 egg yolks
2 tablespoons lemon juice

Melt butter with water, salt and pepper in top of double boiler over simmering water. Beat egg yolks slightly in small bowl. Blend small amount of butter mixture into beaten egg yolks. Add to remaining butter. Beat mixture with rotary beater until thick and smooth. Blend in lemon juice. Serve immediately. Makes one cup

Notes:

MAIN DISHES

PASTA

Asian Pasta Stir-Fry

Sauce:

3 tablespoons sesame seeds, toasted
¼ cup Asian sesame oil
¼ cup mirin (Japanese sweet cooking wine)
¼ cup soy sauce*
3 tablespoons brown sugar

2 teaspoons fish sauce
3 green onions, chopped
3½ ounces fresh shiitake mushrooms, stemmed and sliced

Combine all sauce ingredients except mushrooms in small bowl. Transfer ¼ cup of sauce to medium bowl and stir in mushrooms. Marinate 15-30 minutes.

*La Choy and San-J are gluten free.

Stir-Fry:

1 pound bok choy, washed and sliced
¼ pound fresh sugar snap peas, cut in half
1 carrot, sliced diagonally

16 ounces gluten-free pasta
2 tablespoons vegetable oil
2 shallots, finely chopped

Blanch bok choy, sugar snap peas and carrots in large pot of boiling, salted water 4-5 minutes. Remove vegetables with slotted spoon to colander, and rinse under cold water.

Return water to boil, add pasta and cook until tender, but still slightly firm. Drain and rinse with cold water.

Heat oil in large nonstick skillet and sauté shallots until lightly browned. Add mushroom mixture and sauté until tender. Add remaining sauce, pasta and vegetables, cooking until pasta has absorbed sauce, 3-5 minutes. Serves 6 - 8

MAIN DISHES

Baked Chicken Pasta with Pesto

May be made in two smaller baking pans, freezing one for a later time.

1 pound boneless, skinless organic chicken breast, cut into bite-sized pieces
2 tablespoons extra-virgin olive oil
2 (26-ounce) jars gluten-free tomato and basil pasta sauce
1 (10-ounce) jar basil pesto
1 (15-ounce) container cottage cheese
2 eggs
2 cups mozzarella cheese, freshly grated and divided
1 package frozen chopped spinach, thawed and drained
½ cup Parmesan cheese, freshly grated
1 pound shell or spiral-shaped gluten-free pasta, cooked, drained and rinsed
Gluten-free cooking spray

Preheat oven to 350°. Heat oil in large skillet over medium heat. Add chicken and brown. Add pasta sauce and basil pesto sauce, and heat. Mix cottage cheese, eggs, half of mozzarella cheese, spinach and Parmesan in separate bowl.

Spray 14 x 10-inch casserole. Spread half each of pasta, cottage cheese mixture and chicken sauce, spreading each layer as evenly as possible. Repeat pasta, cottage cheese mixture and remaining chicken sauce, again spreading evenly. Cover casserole with foil and bake 40 minutes. Remove foil, top with remaining mozzarella cheese and bake 5 minutes to melt cheese. Cool 10 minutes. Serves 8 - 10

Notes:

MAIN DISHES

Carbonara Pasta with Prosciutto and Peas

8 ounces gluten-free pasta
1 teaspoon extra-virgin olive oil
4-5 slices prosciutto or bacon
¼ teaspoon red pepper flakes
2 garlic cloves, minced
⅓ cup dry white wine

2 large egg yolks
½ cup chicken broth*
2 cups frozen peas
½ cup water
½ cup Parmesan cheese, freshly grated (optional)

Bring salted water to boil in large pot. Add pasta and cook until al dente, about 8 minutes. Drain and rinse briefly in cold water.

Heat oil in large skillet, add prosciutto and fry until crisp. Remove prosciutto with slotted spoon and coarsely chop. Do not discard fat. Return chopped meat to pan and add red pepper flakes, garlic and wine. Cook 2-3 minutes, stirring well.

Beat egg yolks in small bowl. Warm chicken broth in microwave 10-20 seconds until quite warm, but not boiling. While constantly stirring egg yolks, slowly add chicken broth until combined. This will prevent yolks from cooking when added to pasta.

Place peas in microwave-proof bowl, add water and cover with plastic wrap. Steam in microwave oven until cooked, about 2 minutes. Drain.

Add pasta, egg mixture and peas to skillet. Heat briefly, tossing rapidly until ingredients are combined and egg has cooked. Sprinkle Parmesan cheese over pasta. Serves 4

Pacific Natural Foods Chicken Broth is a gluten-free brand.

Notes:

Main Dishes

Fire-Roasted Tomato and Beef Pasta

8 ounces gluten-free shell or spiral-shaped pasta
2 tablespoons extra-virgin olive oil
½ large sweet onion, chopped
1 garlic clove, minced
1 cup celery, chopped

2 pounds ground beef
2 (14.5-ounce) cans fire roasted diced tomatoes
1-2 tablespoons honey
¾ teaspoon salt

Cook pasta according to package directions. Drain and rinse briefly in cold water and set aside.

Heat oil in large skillet. Sauté onion, garlic and celery until soft. Add ground beef and cook until browned. Add tomatoes, honey and salt. Simmer 10 minutes, stirring occasionally. Add cooked pasta, heat and serve. Serves 6

Italian Chicken Pasta for Two

Great with a green salad and glass of wine

2 boneless, skinless, organic chicken breasts cut into bite-sized pieces
1¼ cup balsamic vinaigrette, divided (see recipe in beginning of Salads)
2 garlic cloves, minced
1 green bell pepper, cut in strips

2 tablespoons extra-virgin olive oil
Salt to taste
Black olives, sliced, to taste
Fresh tomatoes, diced, to taste
8 ounces gluten-free pasta, cooked
Parmesan cheese, freshly grated

Marinate chicken in 1 cup vinaigrette 4-6 hours. Discard vinaigrette. Sauté garlic, green pepper and chicken in oil until chicken is cooked. Toward end of cooking time, add salt and ¼ cup vinaigrette to chicken, and heat through. Add black olives and tomatoes. Remove immediately from heat and cover. Do not cook tomatoes! Serve chicken mixture over hot pasta, and sprinkle with Parmesan cheese. Serves 2

Main Dishes

Lasagna

3 tablespoons extra-virgin olive oil
1 large onion, finely chopped
6-8 garlic cloves, minced
1 pound lean ground beef
1 (28-ounce) can diced tomatoes
1 (12-ounce) can tomato paste
½ cup water
1 tablespoon sugar, or to taste
1½ teaspoons salt
1¼ teaspoons oregano
1¼ teaspoons thyme
½ teaspoon crushed red pepper
2-3 tablespoons parsley flakes
½ teaspoon (heaping) fennel seed
2 bay leaves
8 ounces gluten-free lasagna noodles
Gluten-free cooking spray
2 eggs
1 (15-ounce) container cottage cheese
16 ounces mozzarella cheese, freshly shredded
1 cup Parmesan cheese, freshly grated

Heat oil in 6-quart Dutch oven over medium heat. Add onion and garlic, lower heat, and sauté 10-15 minutes. Raise heat, add beef and sauté until browned. Add tomatoes, tomato paste, water, sugar, salt, oregano, thyme, red pepper, parsley, fennel seed and bay leaves. Heat mixture to boiling, stirring often to prevent sticking. Reduce heat, cover and simmer 30 minutes, stirring occasionally. Remove bay leaves.

Preheat oven to 375°. Cook lasagna noodles, drain and rinse in cold water. Spray 14 x10-inch baking pan and arrange half the lasagna noodles, overlapping to fit. Beat eggs in small bowl and mix in cottage cheese. Spoon half of mixture over noodles. Sprinkle with half of mozzarella and Parmesan cheeses, and top with half of sauce. Repeat layers: noodles, cottage cheese, mozzarella cheese, Parmesan cheese, sauce. Bake 45 minutes. Remove from oven and let cool 10 minutes. Serves 8 - 10

Notes:

MAIN DISHES

Pasta Alfredo

A true taste of Italy

16 ounces gluten-free pasta
½ cup butter, softened
1 cup heavy cream
Freshly ground black pepper to taste
4 ounces Parmesan cheese, freshly grated

Cook pasta according to package directions and drain. In same pan used for pasta, melt butter over low heat. Add hot pasta and stir gently until coated. Add cream and a fair amount of pepper, stirring as cream thickens and clings to pasta. Add Parmesan cheese, stir well and serve. Serves 4 - 6

Pasta Salad

Any gluten-free pasta may be used. Add or remove ingredients as preferred to create a perfect accompaniment to most grilled or broiled meat.

16 ounces gluten-free pasta, cooked
½ pound fresh mushrooms, sliced
1 (4-ounce) can black olives, drained and sliced
1 (7-ounce) jar marinated artichoke hearts, drained and cut into quarters
¾ cup celery, finely sliced
¾ cup green onions, finely sliced with greens
1 small green bell pepper, finely diced
½ cup balsamic vinaigrette (see beginning of Salads for recipe)
2-3 medium tomatoes, diced

Mix all ingredients except tomatoes, toss with vinaigrette, and chill overnight. Add tomatoes just before serving and toss again. Serves 8 - 10

Notes:

MAIN DISHES

Pasta with Artichoke Sauce

¼ cup extra-virgin olive oil
2 tablespoons butter
2 tablespoons rice flour
1 cup chicken broth*
2 garlic cloves, crushed
2 teaspoons lemon juice
1 teaspoon parsley, minced

1 (14-ounce) can artichoke hearts packed in water, drained and quartered
2 tablespoons Parmesan cheese, freshly grated
1 teaspoon capers, drained
8 ounces gluten-free pasta, cooked
Parmesan cheese, freshly grated

Heat oil in large skillet, add butter and melt. Add rice flour and cook, stirring 3 minutes over medium heat. Slowly stir in chicken broth, increase heat and cook 1 minute. Add garlic, lemon juice and parsley, and cook uncovered over low heat 5 minutes. Add artichokes, cheese and capers. Cook uncovered about 8 minutes, stirring occasionally. Toss pasta with hot artichoke sauce. Sprinkle with Parmesan cheese. Serves 2

*Pacific Natural Foods Chicken Broth is a gluten-free brand.

Pasta with Tuna Sauce

Adding sautéed red bell pepper gives spice and color to this light sauce.

4 tablespoons extra-virgin olive oil
2 tablespoons butter
2 large garlic cloves, minced
¾ cup chicken broth*
3 tablespoons white wine or vermouth

2 (7-ounce) cans tuna, drained
Freshly ground black pepper to taste
8 ounces gluten-free pasta, cooked
2 tablespoons fresh parsley, finely chopped
Parmesan cheese, freshly grated

Heat oil and butter in skillet and sauté garlic. Stir in broth and wine, and simmer reducing liquid by one half. Flake tuna into liquid and season with pepper. Heat through. Toss with hot pasta. Garnish with parsley and top with Parmesan cheese. Serve immediately. Serves 2

*Pacific Natural Foods Chicken Broth is a gluten-free brand.

Main Dishes

Sesame Flank Steak with Pasta

The pomegranate juice marinade adds a lively flavor.

⅓ cup soy sauce*
¼ cup sesame oil
½ cup green onions, chopped
4 garlic cloves, minced
½ cup pomegranate juice
2 pounds flank steak, sliced in ½-inch strips

16 ounces gluten-free pasta
2 cups bok choy, Napa cabbage, or green cabbage, chopped
1 (8-ounce) package fresh sugar snap peas
¼ cup sesame seeds, toasted

Marinade:

Combine soy sauce, sesame oil, green onions, garlic and pomegranate juice in container large enough to hold beef strips. Add beef and marinate 10-30 minutes.

Cook pasta according to package directions. Drain, rinse in cold water, and set aside.

Heat large nonstick frying pan or lightly-oiled large pot. Place beef strips in pan with marinade. Cook over medium heat until most beef strips turn brown. Add bok choy and sugar snap peas, cooking 3-4 minutes until vegetables are tender crisp. Add pasta and stir to blend all ingredients. When heated through, remove pan from stove. Sprinkle with sesame seeds and serve. Serves 6

La Choy and San-J are gluten free.

Notes:

MAIN DISHES

Zucchini Pasta

4 tablespoons extra-virgin olive oil
8 garlic cloves, minced
6-8 medium zucchini, diced

Salt
2 servings gluten-free pasta, cooked
Parmesan cheese, freshly grated

Heat oil in large skillet. Add garlic and sauté 5 minutes over low heat. Turn up heat to medium high, add diced zucchini, and salt generously. Sauté 15-20 minutes, stirring often and lowering heat as zucchini softens. Zucchini should be soft, not firm. Serve over cooked pasta with Parmesan cheese. Serves 2

Notes:

MAIN DISHES

VEGETARIAN

Black Beans and Rice Cubano

A quick and spicy meal

2 teaspoons extra-virgin olive oil
1 large green pepper, coarsely chopped
2 garlic cloves, pressed
2 (14.5-ounce) cans black beans, drained
½ teaspoon oregano

3 tablespoons vinegar
3 teaspoons pimiento, minced
2 pepperoncini, minced (optional)
5 cups brown rice, cooked

Heat oil in skillet, add pepper and garlic and sauté until softened. Add all remaining ingredients, except rice. Cover and simmer until heated. Serve over rice. Serves 6

Bok Choy Sesame Stir-Fry

4 tablespoons sesame oil
1 medium carrot, julienned
2 cups red cabbage, thinly sliced
1-2 teaspoons garlic salt, or to taste
2 cups bok choy, chopped

2 medium yellow squash, julienned
1 medium zucchini, julienned
2 tablespoons soy sauce*
Freshly ground black pepper to taste
2 servings rice, cooked

Heat sesame oil in large skillet over medium-high heat. Add carrots and red cabbage, and stir-fry 5 minutes. Sprinkle with half of garlic salt while cooking. Add bok choy, squash and zucchini. Sprinkle with remaining garlic salt, and stir-fry 5 minutes. Remove from heat. Add soy sauce and black pepper, and mix well. Serve over rice. Serves 2

*La Choy and San-J are gluten free.

Notes:

Main Dishes

Cauliflower and Broccoli Stir-Fry

4 tablespoons extra-virgin olive oil
8-10 baby carrots, quartered lengthwise
1 large sweet onion, halved and sliced
Salt to taste
1½-2 teaspoons ground ginger, divided
2-3 cups cauliflower florets
2-3 cups broccoli florets

1 red bell pepper, thinly sliced
2 tablespoons soy sauce*
¼ cup raisins
¼ cup dry roasted, unsalted peanuts
Pepper to taste
4 servings rice, cooked

Prepare all vegetables before starting. Heat oil in large skillet over medium-high heat. Sauté carrots, covering to steam 1 minute. Add onions, sprinkle with salt and ½ teaspoon ginger, and toss. Cover and steam 1 minute. Add cauliflower, sprinkle with salt and ½ teaspoon ginger, and toss. Cover and steam 1-2 minutes. Turn heat down at any time, if vegetables are browning. Add broccoli and red bell pepper. Sprinkle with salt and ½ teaspoon ginger, and toss. Cover and steam 1-2 minutes. When vegetables are cooked, remove from heat and add soy sauce, raisins, peanuts and pepper, and toss. Serve over rice. Any vegetables may be used, add in order according to required cooking time. Serves 4

*La Choy and San-J are gluten free.

Notes:

MAIN DISHES

Italian Vegetable Stew

Delicious use of fresh summer vegetables

1 tablespoon extra-virgin olive oil
1 cup onions, chopped
3-4 garlic cloves, minced
1 red pepper, chopped
2 cups carrots, sliced at an angle
2-3 (14.5-ounce) cans diced tomatoes
1½ teaspoons dried oregano
1 teaspoon salt

½ teaspoon freshly ground black pepper
4 medium zucchini, coarsely diced
4 medium yellow summer squash, coarsely diced
1 cup chicken broth*
1 chicken Herb-ox bouillon cube or packet
Parmesan cheese, freshly grated

Heat oil in soup pot over medium heat. Add onions, lower heat, and sauté 10-15 minutes. Add garlic and red pepper, sautéing 10 minutes. Add carrots, tomatoes, oregano, salt and pepper. Raise heat and bring to boil. Reduce heat to low, cover and simmer 15 minutes. Add zucchini, squash, broth and bouillon. Cook 15-20 minutes. Serve with Parmesan cheese. Serves 6 - 8

*Pacific Natural Foods Chicken Broth is a gluten-free brand.

Notes:

Main Dishes

Spicy Tofu Stir-Fry

Tofu never tasted so good

Seasoning Sauce:

1 tablespoon sugar
3 teaspoons cornstarch
½ teaspoon salt
½ teaspoon crushed red chili pepper

3 tablespoons soy sauce*
1 tablespoon dry sherry
1 tablespoon vinegar
1 tablespoon sesame oil

Mix all ingredients together in small bowl and set aside.

*La Choy and San-J are gluten free.

Stir-Fry:

14 ounces extra-firm tofu, drained, rinsed, and cut into bite-sized pieces
4 tablespoons extra-virgin olive oil, divided
2 slices ginger root, quarter-sized
3 garlic cloves, minced
1 broccoli crown, cut into florets
2 medium zucchini, halved lengthwise and thinly sliced

2 medium yellow squash, halved lengthwise and thinly sliced
1 medium onion, halved and thinly sliced
1 red pepper, thinly sliced
1 (8-ounce) can sliced water chestnuts, drained
½ cup vegetable broth
4 servings rice, cooked

Place tofu pieces on double thickness of paper towels to absorb excess water. Heat 2 tablespoons oil in large non-stick skillet over medium heat. Place tofu pieces in skillet and fry until lightly brown on all sides. Remove to platter and set aside. Wipe skillet dry and return to medium heat. When hot, pour in remaining 2 tablespoons oil. Stir in ginger and garlic, and stir-fry 1 minute. Add broccoli, zucchini, squash, onion, red pepper and water chestnuts, and stir several times. Add broth, cover and steam 2 minutes. Add tofu and seasoning sauce, stirring until sauce thickens. Serve immediately over hot rice. Serves 4

Notes

desserts

Desserts

Gluten-Free Pie Crust
Nutty Crust
Almond Biscotti with Chocolate Topping
Amaretti
Apple Cranberry Pie
Baked Carrot Cake Pudding
Carrot Cake with Lemon Frosting
Cheesecake with Nutty Crust
Chocolate Chip Biscotti
Chocolate-Covered Peanut Butter Eggs
Chocolate Mint Cookies
Chocolate Merlot Truffles
Crème Brûlée
Deep Dish Peach and Blueberry Crisp
Double Chocolate Brownies
Easy Cherry Dessert
Flan
Flourless Chocolate Hummus Cake
Flourless Peanut Butter Cookies
Fresh Strawberry Pie
Frozen Strawberry Delight
Fruit Dip with Cranberry-Orange Relish
Grape-Pineapple Mélange
Grasshopper Dessert Parfait
Jam Bars
Peach Pie
Pecan Pie with Rum
Peanut Brittle
Quick Chocolate Sauce
Quick Key Lime Pie
Raspberry Almond Tart
Raspberry Cream Pie
Rocky Road Popcorn Truffles
Sour Cream Apple Pie
Spice Cookies with Lemon Glaze
Spiced Peaches
Spicy Pumpkin Pie
Strawberries Romanoff
Strawberries with Raspberry Sauce

DESSERTS

Gluten-Free Pie Crust

Following these directions carefully will result in a beautiful single 9 or 10-inch pie crust

1 cup almond flour
½ cup rice flour
¼ cup tapioca flour
¼ cup cornstarch
2 tablespoons sugar

¼ teaspoon salt
7 tablespoons cold butter, cut into pieces
1 tablespoon lemon juice
1 egg

Butter pie plate and set aside. Place flours, cornstarch, sugar and salt in bowl. Blend well. Work butter into flour mixture using pastry blender or fork. Mixture should resemble coarse cornmeal.

Beat together lemon juice and egg in small bowl. Pour over dry ingredients and blend until flour is evenly moistened and forms a ball. Press together firmly, flatten into disk, smooth edges and wrap tightly in plastic wrap. Refrigerate 45 minutes.

Sprinkle water on countertop. Place 12-inch piece of plastic wrap on top and smooth out. Place pastry dough on center and cover with second piece of plastic wrap.

Roll out crust by pushing rolling pin from center of disk to outer edges, rotating around circle to form even 10-inch circle.

Holding onto crust and both pieces of plastic wrap, slide crust onto large cutting board. Peel off top layer of plastic wrap. Place pie pan upside down on center of crust. Slide hand under cutting board and flip crust into pie pan. Press into place and remove remaining piece of plastic wrap. Seal cracks and holes. Trim excess dough to within ½-inch of pan rim. Fold dough under itself along rim and cover thin spots with extra dough.

Make decorative edge by pressing tines of fork against dough to flatten it against rim of pie plate, or flute edges. Chill until ready to use.

Note: Whole Foods makes a very good preformed gluten-free pie crust. It can be found in the freezer section.

Desserts

Nutty Crust

Makes a versatile single 9 or 10-inch pie crust

2½ cups sliced almonds
¼ cup sugar

6 tablespoons butter, melted

Place almonds and sugar in food processor and pulse until finely ground. Place in bowl, add butter and mix well. Put in 9-inch pie plate or springform pan and press firmly to cover bottom and sides. Refrigerate while preparing filling.

Notes:

Desserts

Almond Biscotti with Chocolate Topping

3 eggs
1 cup sugar
½ cup vegetable oil
1 teaspoon vanilla extract
1 teaspoon almond extract
2½ cups almond flour
1 cup rice flour

½ cup tapioca flour or cornstarch
1 teaspoon baking powder
1½ teaspoons xanthan gum
½ cup raw almonds, coarsely chopped
Cinnamon-sugar
Gluten-free vegetable oil or spray

Preheat oven to 325°. Line two large cookie sheets with parchment paper. Blend eggs, sugar, oil and both extracts with electric mixer. In separate bowl, mix together almond flour, rice flour, tapioca flour, baking powder and xanthan gum. Mix well and add to wet ingredients, one scoop at a time. Add chopped almonds.

Oil hands, turn dough onto cutting board and divide into six equal pieces. Roll each piece into long log about 1-1½ inches in diameter. Spray or brush oil on top of each log and sprinkle with cinnamon-sugar. Place three logs on each cookie sheet and bake 28 minutes, or until logs are baked in center, but not browned.

Leaving oven on, remove pans. Cool and remove logs to cutting board using a large spatula. Cut logs diagonally into ¾-inch slices. Return biscotti to baking sheets, laying slices flat and bake 20 minutes longer or until lightly browned. Cool on rack. Makes approximately 6 dozen

Chocolate topping (optional):

6 ounces chocolate chips/bittersweet
    chocolate, coarsely chopped, divided

1 tablespoon corn or canola oil

Place biscotti on waxed paper or cookie sheets in neat rows almost touching each other. Melt 4 ounces chocolate and oil in double boiler over barely simmering water, stirring often. As soon as chocolate has melted, remove from heat. Add 2 remaining ounces of chocolate. Stir until melted. Quickly drizzle warmed chocolate over biscotti in long zigzag lines. Allow biscotti to sit until chocolate hardens, about 30 minutes.

Desserts

Amaretti

A light and delicious end to a meal

¼ teaspoon salt
2 egg whites
1 cup sugar

1 cup blanched almonds, chopped
¾ teaspoon almond extract

Add salt to egg whites and beat until frothy. Add sugar gradually, beating until mixture is stiff, but not dry. Gently fold in almonds and almond extract.

Drop teaspoonfuls of almond mixture onto buttered and floured baking sheet. Shape into ovals, leaving 1 inch between mounds. Let stand 2 hours.

Preheat oven to 375° and bake 12 minutes, or until tops are delicate brown. Makes 25

Notes:

Desserts

Apple Cranberry Pie

1 (9-inch) gluten-free pie crust (See beginning of Desserts for recipe)

Apple and Cranberry Fillings:

2 cups cranberries, washed
¾ cup honey
½ cup orange juice*
Pinch fresh nutmeg
4-6 baking apples, peeled, cored and sliced
¼ cup sugar
2 tablespoons lemon juice
2 tablespoons rice flour
¼ teaspoon cinnamon

Place cranberries, honey, orange juice and nutmeg in pan. Bring to boil, stirring occasionally. Simmer until mixture reduces by one-third, 20-25 minutes. Cool.

Mix apples, sugar, lemon juice, rice flour and cinnamon in separate bowl.

Tropicana is gluten free.

Streusel Topping:

½ cup rice flour
½ cup almond flour
⅓ cup sugar
1½ teaspoons lemon peel, grated
½ cup unsalted butter, chilled

Mix streusel ingredients until crumbly. Spread cooled cranberry filling on crust and cover with apple filling. Sprinkle streusel mixture evenly on top. Cover crust edges with foil and bake 1-1½ hours until lightly browned on top. Serves 6

Notes:

DESSERTS

Baked Carrot Cake Pudding

Carrots never tasted so good!

1 pound carrots, boiled and mashed	½ cup brown sugar, packed
1 cup walnuts, chopped	½ cup butter
1½ teaspoons cinnamon	2 eggs, separated

Preheat oven to 325°. Grease 2½-quart casserole. Mix mashed carrots, walnuts, cinnamon, brown sugar, butter and two beaten egg yolks. Beat egg whites in separate bowl until stiff and fold into mixture. Pour into casserole. Bake 1 hour. Serves 6 - 8

Notes:

DESSERTS

Carrot Cake with Lemon Frosting

⅔ cup pecans
3 cups carrots, peeled
½ cup golden raisins
¾ cup vegetable oil
2 cups brown sugar, loosely packed
4 eggs
1 cup almond flour

1 cup rice flour*
2 teaspoons baking soda
2 teaspoons baking powder
1 teaspoon salt
1 tablespoon cinnamon
½ teaspoon nutmeg
1 teaspoon ground ginger

Preheat oven to 325°. Butter and flour 9 x 13-inch pan. Toast pecans in oven until lightly browned, about 8-10 minutes. Cool pecans, chop, and set aside. Shred carrots in food processor. Coarsely chop raisins. Set both aside.

Place oil, brown sugar and eggs in bowl and blend with electric mixer. In another bowl, mix together flours, baking soda, baking powder, salt, cinnamon, nutmeg and ground ginger. Slowly add flour mixture to oil mixture, blending between each addition. Add pecans, carrots and raisins. Blend briefly and pour into baking pan. Bake 52-55 minutes. Cool cake on rack.

*Sweet rice flour (or sticky rice flour) works very well here.

Lemon Frosting:

1 cup butter, softened
2 cups confectioner's sugar

1 teaspoon vanilla extract
1 teaspoon lemon extract

Put all ingredients in mixing bowl and blend well. Spread on top of cake.

Notes:

DESSERTS

Cheesecake with Nutty Crust

Rich, delicious and sinful

1 Nutty Pie Crust (see beginning of Desserts for recipe)
3 (8-ounce) packages cream cheese, softened
1½ cups sugar
Pinch of salt
4 eggs
1 teaspoon vanilla or almond extract
Dash lemon juice

Press Nutty Pie Crust into bottom of 9-inch springform pan and chill.

Preheat oven to 350°. Blend cream cheese, sugar and salt with mixer. Add eggs one at a time and blend well after each addition. Add vanilla and lemon juice; mix well. Pour into springform pan and bake 50 minutes. Remove from oven and let stand 15 minutes.

Topping:

2 cups sour cream
¼-½ cup sugar
1 teaspoon vanilla extract

Reset oven to 425°. Mix topping ingredients in small bowl. Pour over cheesecake after 15 minutes. Return to oven and bake 10 minutes. Allow to cool and refrigerate overnight. Remove sides of springform pan. Serves 8 - 12

Notes:

Desserts

Chocolate Chip Biscotti

Wonderful with coffee or tea

½ cup rice flour
¼ cup tapioca flour
1 cup almond flour
¼ cup cornstarch
⅔ cup sugar
1 teaspoon baking soda

½ teaspoon xanthan gum
½ teaspoon salt
½ cup milk chocolate, mini-morsels
3 large eggs, beaten
1 teaspoon pure vanilla extract
Gluten-free cooking spray

Preheat oven to 325°. Mix flours, cornstarch, sugar, baking soda, xanthan gum, salt and chocolate chips in medium bowl. Blend in eggs and vanilla. Turn dough onto lightly floured surface. Knead dough eight to ten times. Form dough into 2 x 16-inch log. Place log on cookie sheet coated with cooking spray. Bake 30 minutes. Remove from oven and cool 10 minutes. Place log on cutting board and with serrated knife, cut log diagonally into ½-inch slices. Place slices flat on baking sheet. Reduce heat to 300° and bake 10 minutes. Turn slices over and bake additional 10 -12 minutes until golden. Centers will be slightly soft, but will harden as they cool. Remove from oven and cool on wire rack. Makes 24 biscotti

Notes:

DESSERTS

Chocolate-Covered Peanut Butter Eggs

These chocolate-coated peanut butter eggs are a wonderful seasonal treat.

Peanut Butter Filling:

2 boxes confectioner's sugar
8 ounces chunky peanut butter
1½ cups butter, softened

1 teaspoon vanilla extract
⅛ teaspoon salt

Mix sugar, peanut butter, butter, vanilla and salt together. Shape into balls, then into egg shapes. Dry overnight on waxed paper.

Chocolate Coating:

8 ounces German semi-sweet chocolate   ¼ slice paraffin

The next day, melt chocolate and paraffin in double boiler. Stir mixture well. Dip eggs in chocolate using wire egg holder. Put on waxed paper. Refrigerate. Makes approximately 18 eggs

Notes:

Desserts

Chocolate Merlot Truffles

½ cup heavy cream
12 ounces sweet dark chocolate
¼ cup merlot wine

½ cup unsalted butter, room temperature
½ cup unsweetened powdered cocoa

Simmer cream in small saucepan over low heat until reduced by half. Add chocolate and wine. Stir frequently over low heat until chocolate is melted and smooth. Add butter and mix well. Remove from heat and pour into small bowl. Refrigerate until hard, about one hour. Form mixture into 1-inch balls using teaspoon. Work quickly as truffles will melt. Place powdered cocoa in bowl and roll truffles in cocoa to coat evenly. Store truffles in refrigerator. Hold at room temperature 20 minutes before serving. Makes approximately 18

Chocolate Mint Cookies

A chocolate cookie with a chocolate mint candy melted on top

¾ cup butter
1½ cups brown sugar, firmly packed
2 tablespoons water
2 cups semi-sweet chocolate chips
2 eggs

2½ cups almond flour
1¼ teaspoons baking soda
½ teaspoon salt
2 boxes Andes Crème De Menthe Thins

Melt butter, brown sugar and water in saucepan over low heat. Add chocolate chips, stir until partially melted and remove from heat. Continue to stir until chocolate is completely melted. Pour into large mixing bowl and let cool at room temperature, at least 10 minutes. With mixer on high speed, add eggs one at a time.

Combine flour, baking soda and salt in separate bowl. Blend, slowly adding dry ingredients to chocolate mixture until just incorporated. Cover mixing bowl and chill dough exactly one hour.

Preheat oven to 325°. Line two cookie sheets with parchment paper. Roll rounded tablespoonfuls of dough into balls and place 2 inches apart on cookie sheets. Bake 11-13 minutes until tops of cookies have cracks but are not browned. DO NOT OVERBAKE. Remove from oven and immediately place one Andes mint on each hot cookie. Allow mint to soften, and then spread with small knife. Remove cookies and place on racks to cool completely. Makes approximately 4 dozen cookies

DESSERTS

Crème Brûlée

A classic dessert worthy of an elegant restaurant

8 egg yolks
⅓ cup granulated sugar
2 cups heavy cream

1 teaspoon pure vanilla extract
¼ cup granulated sugar (to caramelize tops)

Preheat oven to 300°. Whisk together egg yolks and sugar in large bowl until sugar dissolves. Add cream and vanilla, and whisk until well blended. Strain mixture through sieve into large bowl.

Divide mixture among 6 ramekins or custard cups. Place in baking pan and add hot water to cover sides half way up ramekins. Bake until set around edges, about 40-50 minutes. Center will still be loose. Remove pan from oven and allow ramekins to cool in water. Remove from water and chill at least 2 hours or up to 2 days.

When ready to serve, sprinkle 2 teaspoons sugar over each ramekin. Caramelize sugar with hand-held torch or put ramekins under broiler until sugar turns golden brown. Serves 6

Notes:

DESSERTS

Deep Dish Peach and Blueberry Crisp

A crisp which combines two favorite summer fruits

¾ cup slivered almonds
1 cup almond flour
2 tablespoons rice flour
2 tablespoons cornstarch
¼ cup brown sugar
¼ teaspoon cinnamon
¼ teaspoon nutmeg

¼ teaspoon salt
5 tablespoons cold butter
6-7 peaches
1½ cups fresh blueberries
1½ tablespoons lemon juice
2 tablespoons honey

Preheat oven to 375°. Place slivered almonds on small baking pan and bake until lightly toasted, about 6 minutes. Allow to cool, chop, and set aside. Butter 9-inch deep-dish pie pan, covering bottom and sides, also set aside.

For topping, place flours, cornstarch, brown sugar, cinnamon, nutmeg and salt in bowl, and combine well. Cut in butter with pastry blender or fork. Add almonds and stir. Mixture will be crumbly.

Peel and slice peaches. Place both fruits in bowl. Add lemon juice and honey, and combine well. Pour fruit mixture into buttered pie pan and evenly spread topping over fruit. Bake 30 minutes or until topping starts to brown. Serves 6 - 8

Notes:

DESSERTS

Double Chocolate Brownies

These flourless chocolate brownies are dense and rich!

8 ounces semisweet or bittersweet chocolate, chopped
¾ cup unsalted butter
1 cup sugar
2 teaspoons vanilla extract

4 large eggs
1 teaspoon salt
2 cups almond flour
1 cup semisweet chocolate chips

Preheat oven to 350º. Butter and flour 13 x 9-inch baking pan. Melt chocolate and butter in double boiler. Stir until mixture is smooth, and remove from heat. Let cool until lukewarm.

Stir in sugar and vanilla. Add eggs, one at a time, stirring well after each addition. Stir in salt and almond flour until just combined. Mix in chocolate chips and pour batter into pan. Smooth top and bake 25-30 minutes, or until center springs back slightly when pressed. Cool brownies completely in pan. Chill pan to make cutting easier. Makes 24 bars

Notes:

Desserts

Easy Cherry Dessert

Crust:

1¾ cups almond flour
⅓ cup sugar

1 teaspoon cinnamon
5 tablespoons butter, melted

Preheat oven to 350º. Butter bottom and sides of 8 x 8-inch baking pan. Place almond flour, sugar and cinnamon in medium-sized bowl, and blend. Add melted butter and mix well. Press crust ingredients evenly into bottom of baking pan. Bake 15 minutes or until crust begins to brown lightly. Remove from oven and cool.

Filling:

1 (21-ounce) can of gluten-free cherry pie filling
2 tablespoons honey

½ teaspoon almond extract
8-ounce container Cool Whip, thawed
¼ cup slivered almonds, toasted

Blend cherry pie filling, honey and almond extract in medium-sized bowl and pour evenly over cooled crust. Cover filling with entire container of Cool Whip. Sprinkle toasted almonds on top. Refrigerate several hours. Serves 8

Notes:

Desserts

Flan

1 cup + 3 tablespoons sugar, divided
2 tablespoons water
2½ cups whole milk

¼ teaspoon vanilla extract
2 large whole eggs
6 egg yolks

Combine 3 tablespoons sugar and water in small pan. Bring to boil over medium heat and boil without stirring until mixture becomes golden brown syrup, about 4 minutes. Pour equal amount brown syrup into each of six 4-ounce ramekins, rotating cups until sides are coated about halfway up. Set cups aside. Pour milk into saucepan, add vanilla, and cook over low heat until small bubbles form along edges, about 7 minutes. DO NOT BOIL MILK.

Preheat oven to 300°. Whisk eggs, egg yolks and sugar in bowl until well-blended. Add small amount hot milk, whisking constantly to prevent yolks from curdling. Add remaining milk little by little while continuing to whisk. Divide custard evenly into prepared cups. Place filled cups in large baking dish and add boiling water to reach about half way up sides of cups. Bake 50-60 minutes, or until set. Centers should jiggle slightly. Remove cups from water and cool to room temperature. Cover and refrigerate 2-6 hours. To serve, run sharp, thin knife blade around inside edge of each cup, and turn onto individual plates. Serves 6

Notes:

DESSERTS

Flourless Chocolate Hummus Cake

Thanks to Chef Darin Sehnert, Culinary Director, 700 Kitchen Cooking School, Savannah, GA for this surprisingly delicious recipe

Gluten-free cooking spray
1 (15-ounce) can garbanzo beans, drained
4 whole eggs
1 teaspoon vanilla extract
1½ cups granulated sugar
½ cup unsweetened cocoa powder

2 tablespoons cornstarch
¾ teaspoon baking powder
¼ teaspoon baking soda
½ teaspoon salt
Confectioner's sugar (optional)

Preheat oven to 350°. Spray inside of 9-inch round cake pan with cooking spray. Cut a parchment paper circle large enough to cover bottom of pan. Place parchment circle in pan and spray paper with cooking spray. Set pan aside.

Place garbanzo beans, eggs and vanilla in bowl of food processor fitted with steel chopping blade. Process until blended and beans are finely puréed.

In medium-sized bowl, combine all dry ingredients except confectioner's sugar, and mix until thoroughly combined and cocoa is well blended with sugar. Be sure that no lumps of cocoa or other ingredients remain. Add dry ingredients to food processor and process about 1 minute, or until completely blended and pureed.

Pour batter into cake pan and bake until toothpick inserted in center comes out clean. Remove from oven and cool about 10 minutes before inverting onto serving plate. Carefully remove paper from top of cake and cool completely. Dust with confectioner's sugar, if desired. Serves 12

Notes:

DESSERTS

Flourless Peanut Butter Cookies

1 cup gluten-free peanut butter (chunky or plain)
1 cup sugar
1 large egg

1 teaspoon baking soda
½ teaspoon vanilla extract
1 cup miniature chocolate chips

Preheat oven to 350°. Mix peanut butter, sugar, egg, baking soda and vanilla together and then add chocolate chips. Mix well. Moisten hands and make tablespoon-sized balls. Place balls on ungreased cookie sheet and bake approximately 12 minutes. Cookies will be soft but puffy and should immediately be transferred to wire rack. Makes approximately 3 dozen cookies

Notes:

DESSERTS

Fresh Strawberry Pie

1 (9-inch) gluten-free pie crust (see beginning of Desserts for recipe)
2 pounds fresh strawberries, hulled and sliced
3 tablespoons cornstarch
½ cup cold water
⅔ cup sugar
1 tablespoon butter
2 tablespoons Grand Marnier liquor or 1 tablespoon lemon juice
Whipped cream or Cool Whip for serving

Preheat oven to 350°. Place pie pan with unbaked crust on heavy baking sheet. Use fork to poke holes in crust. Bake until lightly browned, about 15-20 minutes. Cool crust.

Fill cooled pie crust with sliced berries reserving 1½ cups for puree. Chill filled crust while finishing recipe.

Purée remaining berries in food processor or mash with potato masher to make 1½ cups berry mixture. Add water to berries if necessary to measure 1½ cups.

Combine cornstarch and cold water in small bowl, stirring well. Place berries, sugar and cornstarch mixture in saucepan. Heat in non-reactive saucepan (DO NOT USE ALUMINUM), stirring until berry mixture is thick and clear. Remove from heat and stir in butter and Grand Marnier. Allow mixture to cool 10 minutes. Pour into pie shell, pushing sliced strawberries around to fill all holes and smoothing top with spatula. Chill well and serve with whipped cream or Cool Whip. Serves 6 - 8

Notes:

Desserts

Frozen Strawberry Delight

4 cups strawberries, hulled
1 (14-ounce) can sweetened condensed milk
1 (8-ounce) container Cool Whip, thawed
1 (8.25-ounce) can crushed pineapple, drained
¼ cup lemon juice

Purée strawberries in blender. Set aside. Combine condensed milk and Cool Whip, and mix until blended. Add strawberry purée, pineapple and lemon juice, and blend. Pour mixture into 9 x 13-inch pan and freeze until firm. Remove from freezer 10 minutes before serving. Serves 10

Fruit Dip with Cranberry-Orange Relish

Easy, different and tasty

8 ounces cream cheese, softened
8 ounces sour cream
16 ounces cranberry orange relish*

Mix all ingredients together. Chill until ready to serve. Delicious with any sliced fruit.

*Ocean Spray is gluten free.

Grape-Pineapple Mélange

Refreshing and unique

½ cup white sugar
8 ounces cream cheese
1 teaspoon vanilla extract
1 (12-ounce) can pineapple tidbits, drained
2 pounds seedless grapes
½ cup brown sugar
½ cup pecans, chopped and toasted

Mix sugar with cream cheese and vanilla. Mix pineapple and grapes with cream cheese mixture. Put in 9 x 13-inch pan. Mix brown sugar and nuts, and spread on top. Serves 8

DESSERTS

Grasshopper Dessert Parfait

A cool dessert with an interesting mix of flavors

1 half-gallon gluten-free vanilla ice cream
1 (8-ounce) can crushed pineapple, drained
1 bottle Crème de Menthe

Place two scoops vanilla ice cream in each parfait glass. Put one teaspoon pineapple on top and add another scoop ice cream, topped with another teaspoon pineapple. Pour approximately 2 tablespoons Crème de Menthe over top of each dessert and enjoy.

Jam Bars

½ cup butter
¼ cup powdered sugar
¼ cup brown sugar
1 teaspoon vanilla extract
¼ teaspoon almond extract
1 egg
½ teaspoon baking powder
½ teaspoon ground cinnamon
¾ cup almond flour
¾ cup sweet rice flour
¼ teaspoon salt
¾ cup raspberry or apricot preserves*
¾ cup chopped walnuts or pecans

Preheat oven to 340º (yes, 340º). Butter 9 x 9-inch (or 8 x 10-inch) baking pan.

Place butter and sugars in bowl of electric mixer and beat until soft. Add vanilla, almond extract and egg. Beat until well combined and add dry ingredients, except nuts. Blend well.

Set aside ¾ cup dough and press remainder into baking pan. Smooth dough and fill in all holes. Spread preserves over top. Mix remaining dough with nuts and crumble over preserves. Bake 40 minutes, or until lightly browned on top. Remove from oven, cool and cut into squares. Makes 16 bars

*Polaner All Fruit Spread works well.

DESSERTS

Peach Pie

A true summer favorite that is easy and delicious!

1 (9-inch) gluten-free pie crust recipe (see beginning of Desserts for recipe)
3 cups peaches, peeled and sliced
1 cup heavy cream

3 tablespoons cornstarch
1 cup sugar
½ teaspoon cinnamon

Preheat oven to 400°. Prepare pie crust and fill with sliced peaches. Mix cream, cornstarch, sugar and cinnamon. Pour over fruit.

Bake 10 minutes. Reduce heat to 350°; bake additional 30 minutes or until juices bubble and crust is golden brown. Serves 6-8

Pecan Pie with Rum

The hint of rum gives this pie a wonderful flavor.

1 9-inch gluten-free pie crust (see beginning of Desserts for recipe)
3 large eggs
1¼ cups honey
1 teaspoon vanilla extract
2 tablespoons rum

¼ teaspoon salt
¼ cup salted butter, melted
1½ cups pecans, finely chopped
Slightly sweetened whipped cream or Cool Whip, for serving

Prepare pie crust and refrigerate. Preheat oven to 350°. Break eggs into bowl. Add honey, vanilla, rum, salt and butter. Blend well. Stir in pecans and pour mixture into pie shell. Bake until filling is set but still slightly wobbly in center, about 40 minutes. Serve with whipped cream or Cool Whip. Serves 6

Desserts

Peanut Brittle

Keeps well in a cookie tin for several weeks. Makes a lovely gift.

3 cups sugar
1 cup corn syrup
½ cup water
30 ounces roasted salted peanuts

4 tablespoons butter, salted
2 teaspoons vanilla extract
2 teaspoons baking soda

Measure all ingredients for recipe. Once sugars have heated, it is important to move quickly. Wear long sleeves and protective oven mitts when making recipe. Butter two cookie sheets well on bottoms and sides.

Place sugar, corn syrup and water in large saucepan, allowing plenty of extra room for sugars to expand. Heat sugar mixture on medium-high heat and stir, cooking until frothy and clear. Add peanuts and continue stirring until candy thermometer reads 280°.

Remove pan from heat and immediately add butter, vanilla and baking soda. This will cause peanut brittle to foam and expand rapidly. QUICKLY pour onto cookie sheets before peanut brittle has chance to cool and harden. Use silicone spatula to spread thinly.

Allow peanut brittle to cool and harden. Break into pieces. Store in container at room temperature.

Notes:

DESSERTS

Quick Chocolate Sauce

Perfect on any dessert or with fruit for dipping

½ cup whipping cream
4 ounces sweet baking chocolate, chopped

¼ teaspoon pure vanilla extract

Heat whipping cream in heavy saucepan over medium heat. DO NOT BOIL! Remove from heat. Add chocolate and stir until melted. Stir in vanilla. Makes ¾ cup. Serves 4

Quick Key Lime Pie

For pies with more filling, triple filling ingredients and divide evenly between two crusts.

1 (9-inch) Nutty Pie Crust (see beginning of Desserts for recipe)
3 large egg yolks
½ cup Key lime juice or regular lime juice
1 (14-ounce) can sweetened condensed milk

¼ teaspoon vanilla extract
Pinch salt
Whipped cream for topping
1 lime, thinly sliced

Prepare Nutty Pie Crust and chill. Preheat oven to 350°. Whisk egg yolks until blended. Whisk in lime juice. Add condensed milk, vanilla and salt, whisking until well blended. Pour mixture into crust. Bake 15 minutes. Remove from oven and cool completely on wire rack. Chill until ready to serve. Garnish servings with whipped cream and lime slices. Serves 6 - 8

Notes:

DESSERTS

Raspberry Almond Tart

Pastry:

½ cup rice flour
½ cup tapioca flour
½ cup almond flour
¼ cup sugar

½ cup butter, cut into pieces
2 tablespoons milk or cream
1 egg yolk

Place flours, sugar and butter into small mixing bowl and mix with pastry blender until mixture resembles cornmeal. Add milk to egg yolk, blend and add to flour mixture. Blend until well moistened and mixture forms ball. Knead a few times with heel of hand and shape into flat disk, wrap with plastic wrap and chill about 1 hour. Butter 9-inch tart pan with removable bottom and put into freezer.

Preheat oven to 350°. Remove dough from refrigerator and roll between 2 sheets of plastic wrap. Roll into crust slightly larger than tart pan. Remove one sheet of plastic wrap, lift and flip into pan. Press sides and bottom into place. Chill crust 10 minutes in freezer. Bake 20 minutes. Remove crust from oven and cool on rack for at least 15 minutes. Filling spreads more easily on cool crust. Leave oven on.

Filling:

3 tablespoons butter, softened
¾ cup sugar + 2 teaspoons
3 large egg yolks

¾ cup almond flour
1 teaspoon vanilla extract
2 cups raspberries, washed

Cream butter and sugar in mixing bowl. Add egg yolks, stirring until smooth. Add almond flour and vanilla, and blend until smooth. Spread filling into bottom of prebaked tart shell. Carefully cover with raspberries and sprinkle with 2 teaspoons sugar. Bake 40 minutes. Serves 6 - 8

Notes:

DESSERTS

Raspberry Cream Pie

A delightful frozen dessert that can be made ahead with filling to spare

1 (9-inch) Nutty Pie Crust (see beginning of Desserts for recipe)
16 ounces frozen raspberries, defrosted
2 large egg whites*

½ cup sugar
2 tablespoons lemon juice
1 cup heavy cream

Preheat oven to 350°. Prepare Nutty Pie Crust, bake 12-15 minutes or until slightly browned. Place raspberries in large bowl. Add egg whites, sugar and lemon juice. Beat continuously with electric mixer until soft peaks form. Beat heavy cream in separate bowl until stiff. Fold cream into raspberry mixture. Pour into pie shell and freeze. Pour extra filling into custard cups and freeze for individual servings. Serve directly from freezer. Serves 6 - 8

*Pasteurized eggs are recommended because pie filling is not cooked.

Rocky Road Popcorn Truffles

Little work required for a sweet treat!

Gluten-free cooking spray
1 cup popped popcorn
1 cup mini marshmallows

1 cup salted peanuts
16 ounces semi-sweet baking chocolate

Spray 12 muffin pan lightly. Mix popcorn, marshmallows and peanuts together and divide evenly among muffin cups. Melt chocolate in microwave on high, 45 seconds; stir chocolate. Repeat microwaving, stirring every 15 seconds until chocolate is smooth. Divide chocolate among muffin cups by pouring carefully into center of each cup, filling to top. Gently tap muffin tin on counter to eliminate air bubbles. Place in refrigerator and cool until chocolate is fully set. Unmold. Makes 12

DESSERTS

Sour Cream Apple Pie

1 (9-inch) gluten-free pie crust (see beginning of Desserts for recipe)
1 cup sugar
1 tablespoon flour
1 egg
1 cup sour cream
1 teaspoon vanilla extract
¼ teaspoon salt
5 cups of apples, peeled, cored and sliced

Prepare pie crust and chill. Preheat oven to 350°. Mix sugar and flour, add egg, sour cream, vanilla and salt. Beat until smooth. Add apples and pour into pie crust. Bake 30 minutes.

Topping:

5 tablespoons almond flour
½ cup sugar
¼ cup butter, softened

Mix flour, sugar and butter to resemble bread crumbs. Cover pie with crumb topping and bake 15 minutes longer. Serves 8

Notes:

DESSERTS

Spice Cookies with Lemon Glaze

These cookies have the melt-in-your mouth texture of a butter cookie. The spices and glaze compliment each other beautifully.

8 ounces butter, softened
¾ cup brown sugar
½ teaspoon salt
2 eggs
2 teaspoons vanilla extract
1 cup almond flour
1 cup sweet rice flour

¼ cup tapioca flour
1½ teaspoons cinnamon
1 teaspoon ginger
¼ teaspoon nutmeg
⅛ teaspoon cloves
1 cup raisins
1 cup pecans, toasted and chopped

Preheat oven to 350°. Line two cookie sheets with parchment paper.

Cream butter, sugar and salt in bowl with electric mixer. Add eggs one at a time, beating between additions. Add vanilla and beat well.

Combine flours and spices in small bowl. Add to mixer in three additions, beating in between. Stir in raisins and pecans. Place rounded tablespoons dough on cookie sheet. Bake 15-18 minutes until lightly browned.

Glaze:

1 cup confectioner's sugar
1½ tablespoons butter, very soft
2 tablespoons milk or soymilk

¾ teaspoon vanilla extract
¾ teaspoon lemon extract

Mix glaze ingredients together in small bowl. Remove cookies from oven and immediately place dollop of glaze on each. Makes about 3 dozen

Notes:

DESSERTS

Spiced Peaches

1 (29-ounce) can peach halves
½ cup brown sugar, packed
½ cup cider vinegar
2 teaspoons mixed pickling spice

Drain syrup from peaches into saucepan. Add brown sugar, vinegar and pickling spice. Boil 10 minutes. Add peaches. Simmer gently 5 minutes. Store in glass jars in refrigerator.

Spicy Pumpkin Pie

1 (9-inch) gluten-free pie crust (see beginning of Desserts for recipe)
2 tablespoons butter, melted
1½ cups canned pumpkin
1 teaspoon ginger
1 teaspoon cinnamon
¼ teaspoon nutmeg or mace
¼ teaspoon cloves
2 eggs
2 tablespoons almond flour
½ cup brown sugar, packed
½ cup granulated sugar
2 tablespoons dark molasses
½ teaspoon salt
1 cup milk

Prepare pie crust and chill. Preheat oven to 450°. Blend butter, pumpkin, ginger, cinnamon, nutmeg and cloves in mixing bowl. Beat in eggs, then flour, sugars, molasses and salt. Stir in milk. Pour into pie shell and bake 15 minutes. Reduce oven to 375° and continue baking 45 minutes. Serves 8

Notes:

DESSERTS

Strawberries Romanoff

Easy, but oh so tasty!

4 cups fresh strawberries, hulled
2 navel oranges, peeled and separated into sections

½ cup confectioner's sugar
4 tablespoons Grand Mariner
4 tablespoons cognac

Combine strawberries and orange segments in serving bowl, sprinkle with sugar and add Grand Mariner and cognac. Toss. Chill one hour. Serves 8 - 10

Strawberries with Raspberry Sauce

A refreshing fruit dessert to finish a large meal

4 cups fresh strawberries, hulled, and quartered
¼-⅓ cup Kirsch liqueur

1 (10-ounce) package frozen raspberries, thawed and undrained
2 cups heavy cream, whipped

In small serving bowl, toss strawberries with Kirsch. Purée raspberries in blender. Pour over strawberries, and toss lightly. Refrigerate 2 hours. Spoon cream over individual servings. Serves 5 - 6

Notes:

NOTES

INDEX

A

Almond Biscotti with Chocolate Topping, 186
Amaretti, 187
Appetizers
    Bacon Cheese Spread, 34
    Black Bean Hummus, 34
    Boursin Cheese, 35
    Cheddar Cheese Dip, 35
    Chili Pepper Peanut Dip, 36
    Clam Dip, 36
    Cocktail Swedish Meatballs, 37
    Creamy Taco Dip with Lime, 38
    Curry Spice Dip, 38
    Fresh Fruit Dip, 39
    Fruit Cocktail with Sherry, 39
    Guacamole, 40
    Hot Artichoke Soufflé, 40
    Hot Crab Cocktail Spread, 41
    Hummus with Fresh Vegetables, 41
    Mushroom Pecan Ball, 42
    Pineapple Cream Cheese Spread, 42
    Red Pepper and Garlic Dip, 43
    Salsa Bean Dip, 44
    Sesame Toast Triangles with Garlic, 45
    Shrimp Dip, 45
    Shrimp with Tangy Cocktail Sauce, 46
    Spicy Baked Olives, 46
    Strawberry Cheese Spread, 47
    Sweet and Sour Water Chestnuts, 47
Apple and Orange Ambrosia Salad, 74
Apple Cranberry Pie, 188
Apple-Puffed Pancake Casserole, 20
Apricot Chicken, 134
Artichoke and Avocado Salad with Lemon Garlic Vinaigrette, 75
Artichoke Rice Salad, 76
Asian Pasta Stir Fry, 166
Asian Pork Tenderloins, 151
Asparagus with Shiitake Mushrooms and Tarragon, 96
Avocado Grapefruit Spinach Salad, 76

B

Bacon and Broccoli Quiche, 21
Bacon Cheese Spread, 34
Bacon, Leek and Shiitake Mushroom Quiche, 22
Baked Beans, 97
Baked Carrot Cake Pudding, 189
Baked Ham with Sweet Potatoes and Apples, 152
Baked Chicken with Pesto Pasta, 167
Baked Tuna Melt Sandwiches, 23
Banana Almond Muffins, 24
Basmati Rice with Garlic, 97
Bean Sprout and Mushroom Salad, 77
Beef
    Beef and Turkey Chili with Corn, 123
    Beef Strips Oriental, 124
    Beefy Bean Chowder, 52
    Cocktail Swedish Meatballs, 37
    Fire-Roasted Tomato and Beef Pasta, 169
    Hungarian Goulash, 125

INDEX

Marinated Grilled Flank Steak, 126
Meatloaf with Thyme, 126
Mexican Beef with Rice, 127
Pot Roast Soup with Fennel and Parsnips, 64
Sake-Marinated Filet Mignons, 127
Sesame Flank Steak with Pasta, 173
Simple Meatloaf with Bacon, 128
Sloppy Joes, 128
South-of-the-Boarder Salad, 86
Stuffed Green Peppers, 129
Swedish Meatballs in Cream Cheese Sauce, 130
Texas Beef Chili, 131
Vegetable Beef Soup, 68
Beef and Turkey Chili with Corn, 123
Beef Strips Oriental, 124
Beefy Bean Chowder, 52
Black Bean Hummus, 34
Black Beans and Rice Cubano, 175
Black-Eyed Pea Soup, 53
Blueberry Muffins, 25
Bok Choy Sesame Stir-Fry, 175
Borscht, 54
Boursin Cheese, 35
Breakfast and Brunch
Apple-Puffed Pancake Casserole, 20
Bacon and Broccoli Quiche, 21
Bacon, Leek and Shiitake Mushroom Quiche, 22
Baked Tuna Melt Sandwiches, 23
Banana Almond Muffins, 24
Blueberry Muffins, 25
Cinco de Mayo Omelet, 26
Crabmeat, Broccoli and Mushroom Quiche, 27
Ham and Eggs with Rice, 27
Overnight French Toast, 28
Whole Grain Waffles, 29
Brined Roasted Turkey, 135

Brunswick Stew, 136
Butternut Squash, Cauliflower and Bok Choy, 98

C

Carbonara Pasta with Prosciutto and Peas, 168
Carrot Cake with Lemon Frosting, 190
Cauliflower and Broccoli Sauté, 98
Cauliflower and Broccoli Stir-Fry, 176
Cheddar Cheese Dip, 35
Cheesecake with Nutty Crust, 191
Cheesy Potatoes, 99
Chicken – See Poultry
Chicken and Artichokes, 137
Chicken Barbeque Sauce, 137
Chicken Gumbo, 55
Chicken Pasta Soup, 56
Chicken Parmesan, 138
Chicken Pot Pie, 140
Chicken with Asian Marinade, 139
Chili Pepper Peanut Dip, 36
Chilled Cranberry Soup, 57
Chilled Cucumber Soup, 58
Chilled Strawberry Soup, 59
Chinese Chicken, 141
Chinese Sesame Pasta, 99
Chocolate Chip Biscotti, 192
Chocolate-Covered Peanut Butter Eggs, 193
Chocolate Merlot Truffles, 194
Chocolate Mint Cookies, 194
Cinco de Mayo Omelet, 26
Clam Dip, 36
Cocktail Swedish Meatballs, 37
Cool Rice and Cucumber Salad, 77
Corn Chowder, 59
Crabmeat Pasta Salad, 78

INDEX

Crabmeat, Broccoli and Mushroom Quiche, 27
Cranberry Salad, 78
Cream of Pimiento Soup, 60
Creamy Cauliflower Soup, 61
Creamy Horseradish Potatoes, 100
Creamy Sweet Potatoes, 101
Creamy Taco Dip with Lime, 38
Crème Brûlée, 195
Cucumber Salad, 79
Curried Chicken Casserole, 141
Curried Fruit, 101
Curry Spice Dip, 38

D

Deep Dish Peach and Blueberry Crisp, 196
Desserts
    Almond Biscotti with Chocolate Topping, 186
    Amaretti, 187
    Apple Cranberry Pie, 188
    Baked Carrot Cake Pudding, 189
    Carrot Cake with Lemon Frosting, 190
    Cheesecake with Nutty Crust, 191
    Chocolate Chip Biscotti, 192
    Chocolate-Covered Peanut Butter Eggs, 193
    Chocolate Merlot Truffles, 194
    Chocolate Mint Cookies, 194
    Crème Brûlée, 195
    Deep Dish Peach and Blueberry Crisp, 196
    Double Chocolate Brownies, 197
    Easy Cherry Dessert, 198
    Flan, 199
    Flourless Chocolate Hummus Cake, 200
    Flourless Peanut Butter Cookies, 201
    Fresh Strawberry Pie, 202
    Frozen Strawberry Delight, 203
    Fruit Dip with Cranberry-Orange Relish, 203
    Gluten-Free Pie Crust, 184
    Grape-Pineapple Mélange, 203
    Grasshopper Dessert Parfait, 204
    Jam Bars, 204
    Nutty Crust, 185
    Peach Pie, 205
    Peanut Brittle, 206
    Pecan Pie with Rum, 205
    Quick Chocolate Sauce, 207
    Quick Key Lime Pie, 207
    Raspberry Almond Tart, 208
    Raspberry Cream Pie, 209
    Rocky Road Popcorn Truffles, 209
    Sour Cream Apple Pie, 210
    Spice Cookies with Lemon Glaze, 211
    Spiced Peaches, 212
    Spicy Pumpkin Pie, 212
    Strawberries Romanoff, 213
    Strawberries with Raspberry Sauce, 213
Dressing with Roasted Garlic and Apples, 102

E

Easy Spinach Salad, 80
Easy Cherry Dessert, 198
Emerald Isle Salad, 80

F

Fire Roasted Tomato and Beef Pasta, 169
Fish Chowder, 62
Fish Filets in Foil Packets, 159
Flan, 199
Flourless Chocolate Hummus Cake, 200
Flourless Peanut Butter Cookies, 201

INDEX

French Onion Soup, 62
Fresh Corn Salad, 81
Fresh Fruit Dip, 39
Fresh Strawberry Pie, 202
Frozen Strawberry Delight, 203
Fruit Dip with Cranberry-Orange Relish, 203
Fruit Cocktail with Sherry, 39
Fruits
    Apple and Orange Ambrosia Salad, 74
    Apple Cranberry Pie, 188
    Apple-Puffed Pancake Casserole, 20
    Apricot Chicken, 134
    Avocado Grapefruit Spinach Salad, 76
    Banana Almond Muffins, 24
    Blueberry Muffins, 25
    Chilled Cranberry Soup, 57
    Chilled Strawberry Soup, 59
    Cranberry Salad, 78
    Curried Fruit, 101
    Deep Dish Peach and Blueberry Crisp, 196
    Easy Cherry Dessert, 198
    Fresh Strawberry Pie, 202
    Frozen Strawberry Delight, 203
    Fruit Cocktail with Sherry, 39
    Fruit Dip with Cranberry-Orange Relish, 203
    Grape-Pineapple Mélange, 203
    Mandarin Chicken with Black Beans, 144
    Mandarin Orange Salad, 83
    Peach Pie, 205
    Pineapple Cream Cheese Spread, 42
    Quick Key Lime Pie, 207
    Raspberry Almond Tart, 208
    Raspberry Cream Pie, 209
    Sour Cream Apple Pie, 210
    Spiced Peaches, 212

Strawberry Cheese Spread, 47
Strawberries Romanoff, 213
Strawberries with Raspberry Sauce, 213
Strawberry and Walnut Green Salad, 87
Waldorf Salad, 90

G

Garbanzo Bean and Cucumber Salad, 81
Garlic Mashed Potatoes, 102
Gazpacho, 63
German Sauerkraut, 103
Gluten-Free Bread Crumbs, 96
Gluten-Free Pie Crust, 184
Grape-Pineapple Mélange, 203
Grasshopper Dessert Parfait, 204
Greek Potato Salad, 104
Grilled Chicken Tenders, 142
Grilled Pork Tenderloin with Rosemary and Fennel Seeds, 152
Guacamole, 40

H

Ham and Eggs with Rice, 27
Ham Roll-Ups, 153
Herb and Onion Pork Tenderloin, 154
Hot Artichoke Soufflé, 40
Hot Chicken Salad Casserole, 142,
Hot Chicken Supreme, 143
Hot Crab Cocktail Spread, 41
Hummus with Fresh Vegetables, 41
Hungarian Goulash, 125

I

Italian Chicken Pasta for Two, 169
Italian Green Beans, 104

INDEX

Italian Vegetable Stew, 177

J

Jam Bars, 204

L

Lamb
    Marinated Leg of Lamb, 132
Lasagna, 170
Lemony Orange Roughy, 160
Lentil Salad with Lemon Vinaigrette, 82
Lentil Soup, 63

M

Mandarin Chicken with Black Beans, 144
Mandarin Orange Salad, 83
Marinated Grilled Flank Steak, 126
Marinated Leg of Lamb, 132
Mashed Potatoes Parmesan, 105
Meatloaf with Thyme, 126
Mexican Beef with Rice, 127
Mozzarella, Tomato, Basil Salad, 84
Mushroom Pecan Ball, 42

N

Nutty Brussels Sprouts, 105
Nutty Crust, 185

O

Old-Fashioned Potato Salad, 106
Orange Honey-Glazed Carrots, 106
Oriental Slaw, 85
Oven-Roasted Broccoli and Cauliflower, 107
Oven-Roasted Sweet Potatoes, 107
Overnight French Toast, 28

P

Pan Gravy for Poultry, 133
Pasta
    Asian Pasta Stir-Fry, 166
    Baked Chicken Pesto Pasta, 167
    Carbonara Pasta with Prosciutto and Peas, 168
    Chinese Sesame Pasta, 99
    Crabmeat Pasta Salad, 78
    Fire Roasted Tomato and Beef Pasta, 169
    Italian Chicken Pasta for Two, 169
    Lasagna, 170
    Pasta Alfredo, 171
    Pasta Salad, 171
    Pasta with Artichoke Sauce, 172
    Pasta with Tuna Sauce, 172
    Sesame Flank Steak with Pasta, 173
    Zucchini Pasta, 174
Peach Pie, 205
Peanut Brittle, 206
Pecan Pie with Rum, 205
Peppers and Onion Sauté, 108
Pineapple Cream Cheese Spread, 42
Pork
    Asian Pork Tenderloins, 151
    Bacon Cheese Spread, 34
    Baked Ham with Sweet Potatoes and Apples, 152
    Carbonara Pasta with Prosciutto and Peas, 168
    Grilled Pork Tenderloin with Rosemary and Fennel Seeds, 152
    Ham and Eggs with Rice, 27
    Ham Roll-Ups, 153
    Herb and Onion Pork Tenderloin, 154
    Pork Chops with Lime Sauce, 154
    Pork Chops with Tropical Sauce, 155

INDEX

Pork Loin Roast with Allspice and Thyme, 156
Pork Medallions in Vermouth with Coriander, 157
Raisin Sauce for Ham, 158
Pot Roast Soup with Fennel and Parsnips, 64

Potatoes
Cheesy Potatoes, 99
Creamy Horseradish Potatoes, 100
Creamy Sweet Potatoes, 101
Garlic Mashed Potatoes, 102
Greek Potato Salad, 104
Mashed Potatoes Parmesan, 105
Old-Fashioned Potato Salad, 106
Oven-Roasted Sweet Potatoes, 107
Roasted Potatoes with Garlic and Thyme, 110
Sweet Potato Risotto, 114
Sweet Potatoes with Orange Glaze, 115

Poultry
Apricot Chicken, 134
Baked Chicken Pesto Pasta, 167
Beef and Turkey Chili with Corn, 123
Brined Roasted Turkey, 135
Brunswick Stew, 136
Chicken and Artichokes, 137
Chicken Barbeque Sauce, 137
Chicken Gumbo, 55
Chicken Pasta Soup, 56
Chicken Parmesan, 138
Chicken Pot Pie, 140
Chicken with Asian Marinade, 139
Chinese Chicken, 141
Curried Chicken Casserole, 141
Grilled Chicken Tenders, 142
Hot Chicken Salad Casserole, 142
Hot Chicken Supreme, 143
Italian Chicken Pasta for Two, 169
Mandarin Chicken with Black Beans, 144

Pan Gravy for Poultry, 133
Southwestern Chicken, 145
Specialty Chicken with Artichokes, 146
Stir-Fry Chicken, 147
Sweet and Sour Chicken, 148
Tropical Chicken Salad, 89
Turkey Salad, 89
Turkey Soup with Sugar Snap Peas, 67
Turkey Tenderloins, 148
White Chili, 149
Zesty Chicken and Sausage Stew, 150

Q

Quiches
Bacon and Broccoli Quiche, 21
Bacon, Leek and Shiitake Mushroom Quiche, 22
Crabmeat, Broccoli and Mushroom Quiche, 27
Quick Chocolate Sauce, 207
Quick Key Lime Pie, 207

R

Raisin Sauce for Ham, 158
Raspberry Almond Tart, 208
Raspberry Cream Pie, 209
Red Cabbage, 109
Red Pepper and Garlic Dip, 43

Rice
Artichoke Rice Salad, 76
Basmati Rice with Garlic, 97
Black Beans and Rice Cubano, 175
Cool Rice and Cucumber Salad, 77
Mexican Beef with Rice, 127
Shrimp and Scallops with Wild Rice, 161
White Rice with Mushrooms, 115
White Rice with Peas, 116
Roasted Asparagus with Parmesan, 110

INDEX

Roasted Potatoes with Garlic and Thyme, 110
Rocky Road Popcorn Truffles, 209

S

Sake-Marinated Filet Mignons, 127
Salad with Hot Bacon Dressing, 86
Salads
    Apple and Orange Ambrosia Salad, 74
    Artichoke and Avocado Salad with Lemon Garlic Vinaigrette, 75
    Artichoke Rice Salad, 76
    Avocado Grapefruit Spinach Salad, 76
    Bean Sprout and Mushroom Salad, 77
    Cool Rice and Cucumber Salad, 77
    Crabmeat Pasta Salad, 78
    Cranberry Salad, 78
    Cucumber Salad, 79
    Easy Spinach Salad, 80
    Emerald Isle Salad, 80
    Fresh Corn Salad, 81
    Garbanzo Bean and Cucumber Salad, 81
    Greek Potato Salad, 104
    Lentil Salad with Lemon Vinaigrette, 82
    Mandarin Orange Salad, 83
    Mozzarella, Tomato, Basil Salad, 84
    Old-Fashioned Potato Salad, 106
    Oriental Slaw, 85
    Pasta Salad, 171
    Salad with Hot Bacon Dressing, 86
    Shrimp Salad, 163
    South-of-the-Border Salad, 86
    Strawberry and Walnut Green Salad, 87
    Tangy Summer Salad, 88
    Tropical Chicken Salad, 89
    Turkey Salad, 89
    Waldorf Salad, 90
Salsa Bean Dip, 44
Sautéed Green Beans and Onions, 111

Sautéed Shrimp and Mushrooms, 160
Savory Zucchini with Bacon, 111
Scalloped Corn, 111
Seafood
    Baked Tuna Melt Sandwiches, 23
    Clam Dip, 36
    Crabmeat, Broccoli and Mushroom Quiche, 27
    Crabmeat Pasta Salad, 78
    Fish Chowder, 62
    Fish Filets in Foil Packets, 159
    Hot Crab Cocktail Spread, 41
    Lemony Orange Roughy, 160
    Pasta with Tuna Sauce, 172
    Sautéed Shrimp and Mushrooms, 160
    Shrimp and Crab Bisque, 65
    Shrimp and Scallops with Wild Rice, 161
    Shrimp Curry, 162
    Shrimp Dip, 45
    Shrimp Provençal, 163
    Shrimp Salad, 163
    Shrimp with Roasted Red Pepper Cream, 164
    Shrimp with Tangy Cocktail Sauce, 46
    Steamed Salmon with Hollandaise Sauce, 165
Sesame Flank Steak with Pasta, 173
Sesame Toast Triangles with Garlic, 45
Shrimp and Crab Bisque, 65
Shrimp and Scallops with Wild Rice, 161
Shrimp Curry, 162
Shrimp Dip, 45
Shrimp Provençal, 163
Shrimp Salad, 163
Shrimp with Roasted Red Pepper Cream, 164
Shrimp with Tangy Cocktail Sauce, 46

INDEX

Sides
    Asparagus with Shiitake Mushrooms and Tarragon, 96
    Baked Beans, 97
    Basmati Rice with Garlic, 97
    Butternut Squash, Cauliflower and Bok Choy, 98
    Cauliflower and Broccoli Sauté, 98
    Cheesy Potatoes, 99
    Chinese Sesame Pasta, 99
    Creamy Horseradish Potatoes, 100
    Creamy Sweet Potatoes, 101
    Curried Fruit, 101
    Dressing with Roasted Garlic and Apples, 102
    Garlic Mashed Potatoes, 102
    German Sauerkraut, 103
    Gluten-Free Bread Crumbs, 96
    Greek Potato Salad, 104
    Italian Green Beans, 104
    Mashed Potatoes Parmesan, 105
    Nutty Brussels Sprouts, 105
    Old-Fashioned Potato Salad, 106
    Orange Honey-Glazed Carrots, 106
    Oven-Roasted Broccoli and Cauliflower, 107
    Oven-Roasted Sweet Potatoes, 107
    Peppers and Onion Sauté, 108
    Red Cabbage, 109
    Roasted Asparagus with Parmesan, 110
    Roasted Potatoes with Garlic and Thyme, 110
    Sautéed Green Beans and Onions, 111
    Savory Zucchini with Bacon, 111
    Scalloped Corn, 111
    Simple Yellow Squash, 112
    Spinach with Raisins and Pine Nuts, 112
    Steamed Butternut Squash and Fennel, 113
    Sweet and Sour Cabbage, 113
    Sweet Potato Risotto, 114
    Sweet Potatoes with Orange Glaze, 115
    White Rice with Mushrooms, 115
    White Rice with Peas, 116
    Zucchini and Sweet Onion Sauté, 116
Simple Meatloaf with Bacon, 128
Sloppy Joes, 128
Soups
    Beefy Bean Chowder, 52
    Black-Eyed Pea Soup, 53
    Borscht, 54
    Chicken Gumbo, 55
    Chicken Pasta Soup, 56
    Chilled Cranberry Soup, 57
    Chilled Cucumber Soup, 58
    Chilled Strawberry Soup, 59
    Corn Chowder, 59
    Cream of Pimiento Soup, 60
    Creamy Cauliflower Soup, 61
    Fish Chowder, 62
    French Onion Soup, 62
    Gazpacho, 63
    Lentil Soup, 63
    Pot Roast Soup with Fennel and Parsnips, 64
    Shrimp and Crab Bisque, 65
    Tailgate Soup, 66
    Turkey Soup with Sugar Snap Peas, 67
    Vegetable Beef Soup, 68
Sour Cream Apple Pie, 210
South-of-the-Border Salad, 86
Southwestern Chicken, 145
Specialty Chicken with Artichokes, 146
Spice Cookies with Lemon Glaze, 211
Spiced Peaches, 212
Spicy Baked Olives, 46
Spicy Pumpkin Pie, 212
Spicy Tofu Stir-Fry, 178
Spinach with Raisins and Pine Nuts, 112
Steamed Butternut Squash and Fennel, 113

INDEX

Steamed Salmon with Hollandaise Sauce, 165
Stir-Fry Chicken, 147
Strawberries Romanoff, 213
Strawberries with Raspberry Sauce, 213
Strawberry and Walnut Green Salad, 87
Strawberry Cheese Spread, 47
Stuffed Green Peppers, 129
Swedish Meatballs in Cream Cheese Sauce, 130
Sweet and Sour Cabbage, 113
Sweet and Sour Chicken, 148
Sweet and Sour Water Chestnuts, 47
Sweet Potato Risotto, 114
Sweet Potatoes with Orange Glaze, 115

T

Tailgate Soup, 66
Tangy Summer Salad, 88
Texas Beef Chili, 131
Tropical Chicken Salad, 89
Turkey - see Poultry
Turkey Salad, 89
Turkey Soup with Sugar Snap Peas, 67
Turkey Tenderloin, 148

V

Vegetable Beef Soup, 68
Vegetables
    Artichoke and Avocado Salad with Lemon Garlic Vinaigrette, 75
    Artichoke Rice Salad, 76
    Avocado Grapefruit Spinach Salad, 76
    Asparagus with Shiitake Mushrooms and Tarragon, 96
    Baked Beans, 97
    Basmati Rice with Garlic, 97
    Bean Sprout and Mushroom Salad, 77
    Black Bean Hummus, 34
    Black Beans and Rice Cubano, 175
    Bok Choy Sesame Stir-Fry, 175
    Butternut Squash, Cauliflower and Bok Choy, 98
    Cauliflower and Broccoli Sauté, 98
    Cauliflower and Broccoli Stir-Fry, 176
    Cheesy Potatoes, 99
    Corn Chowder, 59
    Cream of Pimiento Soup, 60
    Creamy Cauliflower Soup, 61
    Creamy Horseradish Potatoes, 100
    Creamy Sweet Potatoes, 101
    Dressing with Roasted Garlic and Apples, 102
    Easy Spinach Salad, 80
    Fresh Corn Salad, 81
    Garlic Mashed Potatoes, 102
    Garbanzo Bean and Cucumber Salad, 81
    Gazpacho, 63
    German Sauerkraut, 103
    Greek Potato Salad, 104
    Hot Artichoke Soufflé, 40
    Hummus with Fresh Vegetables, 41
    Italian Green Beans, 104
    Italian Vegetable Stew, 177
    Lentil Salad with Lemon Vinaigrette, 82
    Lentil Soup, 63
    Mashed Potatoes Parmesan, 105
    Mozzarella, Tomato, Basil Salad, 84
    Mushroom Pecan Ball, 42
    Nutty Brussels Sprouts, 105
    Old-Fashioned Potato Salad, 106
    Orange Honey-Glazed Carrots, 106
    Oriental Slaw, 85
    Oven-Roasted Broccoli and Cauliflower, 107
    Oven-Roasted Sweet Potatoes, 107

INDEX

Peppers and Onion Sauté, 108
Red Cabbage, 109
Red Pepper and Garlic Dip, 43
Roasted Asparagus with Parmesan, 110
Roasted Potatoes with Garlic and Thyme, 110
Sautéed Green Beans and Onions, 111
Savory Zucchini with Bacon, 111
Scalloped Corn, 111
Simple Yellow Squash, 112
Spinach with Raisins and Pine Nuts, 112
Steamed Butternut Squash and Fennel, 113
Stuffed Green Peppers, 129
Sweet and Sour Cabbage, 113
Sweet Potato Risotto, 114
Sweet Potatoes with Orange Glaze, 115
Tangy Summer Salad, 88
White Rice with Mushrooms, 115
White Rice with Peas, 116
Zucchini and Sweet Onion Sauté, 116
Zucchini Pasta, 174

Vegetarian
Black Beans and Rice Cubano, 175
Bok Choy Sesame Stir-Fry, 175
Cauliflower and Broccoli Stir-Fry, 176
Italian Vegetable Stew, 177
Pasta Alfredo, 171
Pasta Salad, 171
Spicy Tofu Stir-Fry, 178
Zucchini Pasta, 174

W

Waldorf Salad, 90
White Chili, 149
White Rice with Mushrooms, 115
White Rice with Peas, 116
Whole Grain Waffles, 29

Z

Zesty Chicken and Sausage Stew, 150
Zucchini and Sweet Onion Sauté, 116
Zucchini Pasta, 174

Authors of "gluten free By Design": top row: Pat Zungoli, Kitty Neckerman, Wendy Longo; bottom row: Susan Wagener, Debbie Zungoli

Order Additional Copies
Gluten free By Design

Purchase additional copies of ***gluten free By Design*** by returning an order form and your check or money order to:

        Red, White and Tea, LLC
        P.O. Box 147
        Pendleton, SC 29670

Send ____ copies of ***gluten free By Design*** at $25.00 per copy to cover book, shipping and handling. SC residents add $1.17 (per copy) for sales tax. Enclosed is a check or money order for $_____.

Name: _____

Address: _____

City: _____ State: _____ Zip Code: _____

Phone number: _____

Send ____ copies of ***gluten free By Design*** at $25.00 per copy to cover book, shipping and handling. SC residents add $1.17 (per copy) for sales tax. Enclosed is a check or money order for $_____.

Name: _____

Address: _____

City: _____ State: _____ Zip Code: _____

Phone number: _____

Or order on line at www.glutenfreebydesign.com